An Introduction to Regional Englishes

REFERENCE
ONLY

Edinburgh Textbooks on the English Language

TITLES IN THE SERIES INCLUDE

An Introduction to English Syntax
Jim Miller

An Introduction to English Phonology
April McMahon

An Introduction to English Morphology: Words and Their Structure
Andrew Carstairs-McCarthy

An Introduction to International Varieties of English
Laurie Bauer

An Introduction to Middle English
Jeremy Smith and Simon Horobin

An Introduction to Old English
Richard Hogg

An Introduction to Early Modern English
Terttu Nevalainen

An Introduction to English Semantics and Pragmatics
Patrick Griffiths

An Introduction to English Sociolinguistics
Graeme Trousdale

An Introduction to Late Modern English
Ingrid Tieken-Boon van Ostade

An Introduction to Regional Englishes: Dialect Variation in England
Joan Beal

An Introduction to English Phonetics
Richard Ogden

An Introduction to Regional Englishes

Dialect Variation in England

Joan C. Beal

Edinburgh University Press

© Joan C. Beal, 2010

Edinburgh University Press Ltd
22 George Square, Edinburgh

www.euppublishing.com

Reprinted 2011

Typeset in Janson
by Norman Tilley Graphics Ltd, and
printed and bound in Great Britain by
CPI Antony Rowe, Chippenham and Eastbourne

A CIP record for this book is available from the British Library

ISBN 978 0 7486 2116 3 (hardback)
ISBN 978 0 7486 2117 0 (paperback)

Contents

Figures and tables

Figures

Tables

Acknowledgements

I am immensely grateful to Heinz Giegerich for encouraging me to write this in the first place, and to Esme Watson and the team at Edinburgh University Press for their patience and support. I am also grateful to Derek Britton for his helpful and constructive comments.

Thanks to Chris Montgomery for compiling the map of locations (Figure 0.1). Thanks to the following for permission to reproduce material: Cambridge University Press (Figure 4.2); Carmen Llamas (Figures 4.3 and 6.1); Lourdes Burbano-Elizondo (Figure 6.1, Table 6.2 and the identity questionnaire accompanying the exercise for Chapter 6). Thanks to Emma Moore for permission to use the table of grammatical features which accompanies the exercise for Chapter 3.

Thanks to the University of Sheffield for granting me a semester's research leave in 2008–9, which allowed me to make considerable progress on this book, and to the colleagues in the School of English Literature, Language and Linguistics who took up my duties in this period.

As always, I am grateful to my husband Ninian and my daughters Madeleine and Alice for their support and forbearance while I was writing this book. Special thanks to my future son-in-law Matt for the constant supply of hot drinks he provided to keep me going.

Figure 0.1 Map of locations mentioned in this book. *Source:* 2001 Census Output Area Boundaries. Crown copyright 2003.

Abbreviations

ALE	Atlas Linguarum Europae
BNC	British National Corpus
CSU	Corpus of Sheffield Usage
EDD	*English Dialect Dictionary*
FRED	Freiburg Regional English Dialects
HMI	Her Majesty's Inspectors
IDQ	identity questionnaire
IPA	International Phonetic Alphabet
ISA	Index of Sunderland Affiliation
NECTE	Newcastle Electronic Corpus of Tyneside English
OED	*Oxford English Dictionary*
RP	Received Pronunciation
SED	Survey of English Dialects
SRN	Sense Relation Network Sheet
StE	Standard English

1 Introduction

1.1 English dialects in the twenty-first century

The first decade of the twenty-first century is an interesting time to be writing a book about local and regional language variation in England. On the one hand, we are constantly hearing that regional dialects are dying out, to be replaced by what has come to be known as 'Estuary English', but on the other hand, public interest in regional dialects is keener than ever. From 2005, the BBC Voices project invited listeners and readers of their website (www.bbc.co.uk/voices) to contribute their words for certain concepts, and to take part in activities such as an accent recognition test. By the end of October 2006, 79,302 users of the website had submitted a total of 40,751 words to the Word Map and 90,175 users had started the Accent Recognition test up (BBC Voices team: email communication, 3 November 2006).

In some ways, this apparent contradiction is not surprising: the up-surge of interest in dialects at the very point at which they are perceived to be disappearing could be seen as a rearguard action, similar to the reaction against globalisation and 'McDonaldisation' by those who advocate using local shops rather than out-of-town supermarkets. Indeed, the charitable organisation Common Ground, which campaigns for the preservation of 'local distinctiveness', explicitly makes this connection. Noting that 'we all know too many high streets which look the same, housing estates which could be anywhere, fields which have lost both history and birdsong or festivals which have no authenticity', they include in their definition of elements of 'local distinctive-ness' those which are 'ephemeral and invisible', notably 'customs, dialects, celebrations, names, recipes, spoken history, myths, legends and symbols' (www.commonground.org.uk/distinctiveness/d-index.html; see also Clifford and King 2006). Likewise, UNESCO's Convention for the Safeguarding of Intangible Cultural Heritage includes in its definition of the latter 'oral traditions and expressions, including

1

language as a vehicle of the intangible cultural heritage'. The UNESCO statement then goes on to declare that 'many elements of the ICH are endangered, due to effects of globalization' (www.unesco.org/culture/ich_convention/index.php?pg=00003).

Statements such as these seem to presuppose that local dialects are 'endangered' and need to be safeguarded or preserved, and evidence of the geographical diffusion of linguistic features, especially those associated with 'Estuary English', is often seized upon by journalists to provide alarmist copy. Gillian Harris, writing in *The Times* (20 February 1999) under the headline 'Glasgow puts the accent on Estuary', reports on a sociophonetic study conducted by Jane Stuart-Smith:

> Early indications suggest that traditional Glaswegian will struggle to survive. The researchers say that the insidious spread of Estuary English, which has its roots in Essex and Kent, has been felt in such cities as Derby, Newcastle and Hull.

In fact, the researchers said no such thing, and would certainly not have used such a loaded term as 'insidious', but reports of 'traditional' dialects 'struggling to survive' are commonplace.[1]

Although such reports are often sensationalised by the press, it cannot be denied that there is extensive evidence for change leading to loss of distinctiveness in dialects. The 'blurb' for a recent volume on this subject states that 'due to increased mobility in recent years, European dialects have "levelled", making it difficult to distinguish a native of Reading from a native of London, or a native of Bonn from a native of Cologne' (Auer et al. 2005, back cover). Although the collection deals with both convergence and divergence of dialects, it is the former that is foregrounded as the 'hot' topic.

1.2 The 'death of dialects' in the nineteenth century

We will discuss diffusion and levelling, the two processes whereby distinctions between dialects are eroded, in Chapter 5, but it is worth stating at the outset that premature reports of the death of dialects are nothing new. Many of the urban dialects which will be discussed in later chapters are themselves the product of the same levelling and diffusing processes in the late eighteenth and early nineteenth centuries, when the enclosure of common land, the mechanisation of agriculture and the Industrial Revolution provided the 'push' and 'pull' factors which caused people to move from the countryside into rapidly expanding industrial towns and cities. The members of the English Dialect Society, founded in 1873, concentrated their efforts on recording and preserving what they regarded as the 'pure' dialect of rural areas, before it disappeared. The greatest projects sponsored by the English Dialect Society were Joseph Wright's *English Dialect Dictionary* (1898–1905) and *English Dialect Grammar* (1905). In the preface to the latter, Wright states:

> There can be no doubt that pure dialect speech is rapidly disappearing even in country districts, owing to the spread of education, and to modern facilities of intercommunication. The writing of this grammar was begun none too soon, for had it been delayed another twenty years, I believe it would by then be quite impossible to get together sufficient pure dialect material to enable anyone to give even a mere outline of the phonology of our dialects as they existed at the close of the nineteenth century. (1905: iv–v)

In a letter written in 1895 eliciting funds for the *English Dialect Dictionary*, W. W. Skeat, Professor of Anglo-Saxon in the University of Cambridge, stressed the urgency of the project: 'The dialects are dying, and the competent helpers who understand them are waxing old. In a few years it will be too late' (cited in Görlach 1999: 213). The factors mentioned by Wright, 'education' and 'modern facilities of communication', would certainly have affected the traditional dialects spoken in English villages. Universal elementary education was introduced in 1870, with the result that every child was given some schooling. There is evidence that features of local accent and dialect were discouraged by schoolteachers anxious to impose Standard English (StE)/Received Pronunciation (RP), and that this was government policy. According to John Honey, Her Majesty's Inspectors of Schools (HMIs) after 1870 increasingly stressed in their reports the need to eradicate local accents and dialects. In 1886, one HMI advocated the 'kindly and judicious use of ridicule' by teachers encountering the 'inarticulate utterances' of children in South Yorkshire, and in 1894, student teachers at Armstrong College, University of Durham, were advised that they would need help to 'overcome the peculiarities of local pronunciation' (Honey 1988: 221–2).

Improvements in transport, notably the development of the rail network from the 1830s onwards, led to the face-to-face contact between speakers of different dialects which, in modern studies of linguistic variation and change, has been shown to cause both levelling and diffusion (Kerswill 2003). A large number of dictionaries and glossaries of individual dialects were produced in the late nineteenth and early twentieth centuries, and the authors of these all repeat the same refrain: their task is to preserve or at least record a moribund dialect, and the twin factors responsible for that dialect's imminent demise are education and the railways. Here are just a few examples of such comments:

The march of education must sooner or later trample down and stamp out anything like distinctive provincial dialect in England; but when this result shall have been effected, much that is really valuable will be lost to our language, unless an effort is promptly made to collect and record words which, together with the ideas which first rendered them necessary, are rapidly falling into disuse. (Parish 1875: i)

There can scarcely be a doubt that the genuine South Lancashire dialect, the Folk-Speech of our grandfathers and grandmothers, is fast dying out so far as oral communication is concerned. Railways and compulsory state education are making havoc of the old words. (Taylor 1901: v)

Railways and certificated schoolmasters, despite their advantages, are making sad havoc of much that is interesting and worth preserving in the mother tongue of the people. This is to be regretted. It is with the object of collecting any such relics of the past, which would otherwise be doomed to oblivion, that I make the following appeal to my brother Yorkshiremen. (Morris 1892: v)

Although dialects were certainly changing in this period, and new urban dialects evolving, some of the features thought to be doomed have proved resistant to the forces of standardisation. R. O. Heslop, writing in the introduction to his *Northumberland Words*, repeats the refrain that 'the tendency to assimilate the form of the dialect with the current English of the schools is increasing' (1892: xx–xxi). However, one of the features which he expected to disappear was the use of the objective pronoun as part of a compound subject. The example which Heslop provides, 'me and me marrow ["workmate"] wis gannin ti work', also provides an example of the 'Northern Subject Rule', whereby in Scottish and Northern English dialects, compound subjects take a singular verb. As we shall see in Chapter 3, neither of these features has disappeared, despite continuing stigmatisation and pressure from the 'current English of the schools'.

1.3 English dialects and dialectology in the twentieth century

The twentieth century saw the introduction of broadcasting, and the BBC, with its insistence on RP-speaking announcers, was added to the demonology of dialectologists. By the time Harold Orton initiated the Survey of English Dialects (SED) in 1948, even the remotest hill farmer would have been exposed to 'BBC English'. Educationalists continued to emphasise the need to instil Standard English: the report of the Newbolt

Committee advocated 'systematic training in the use of Standard English' to correct the 'evil habits of speech contracted in home and street' (1921: 59). Harold Orton, discussing the decline of the reduced definite article [t] in the South Durham village of Byers Green, notes 'the fact that [t] is rapidly dying out is doubtless one of the immediate results of our educational system' (1933: xvii). In an address to the Yorkshire Dialect Society on the subject of 'the dialects of Northumberland', Orton warns his audience that 'judged historically, these vernaculars have deteriorated considerably' and goes on to enumerate 'the factors that have contributed to the disintegration of dialect':

> Chief among these is Education: the law making attendance at school compulsory has no doubt sounded the death-knell of the old folk-speech. But we may not ignore the growth of industry, with its consequent shifting of populations. ... That the presence of these imported workmen could have had no appreciable influence on the local dialects is scarcely credible. Then again, there is the influence of newspapers and books, and more latterly that of broadcasting. Further, there are the enormously increased facilities for intercommunication, even between the most remote districts: no longer are our country populations satisfied with the amenities of their villages and content to remain at home. (1930: 19–20)

Quite apart from these potential standardising influences, World War II disrupted the social networks of cities, towns and villages: servicemen came into close contact with comrades from different parts of the country, and, indeed, different parts of the English-speaking world, whilst their children might have been evacuated to rural areas from cities considered targets for bombing raids. All these factors were recognised by Orton, whose aim in conducting the SED was to preserve a record of 'traditional vernacular, genuine and old' (1960: 332), and by Stanley Ellis, whose account of his fieldwork for the SED echoes Wright's sense of having recorded the dialects 'just in time':

> First of all, the work must be done as speedily as possible. The effect of the upheaval of two world wars, the broadening of national education and the improvement in transport and various other factors are quickly breaking down the social and geographical barriers, and in fact with the younger generation, have already done so. Very often in visiting a village to-day, a fieldworker will be told that he has arrived just too late, for old so-and-so, who was the right man to answer questions about old times, has recently died, and there are no more natives like him left. (1953: 12)

1.4 Dialects old and new

Of course, the SED had a historical focus: the aim was to trace the reflexes of Middle English variants in the 'traditional' dialects of the twentieth century, so it is not surprising that Orton and his fieldworkers were alarmed at the potential disruption to this line of descent caused by the social factors outlined above. However, what was happening at the various points in history at which dialectologists sounded alarm bells was not the *loss* of dialects so much as *change*, leading to new dialects. Chris Montgomery, in a study of perceptions of dialect differences within the North of England (2006), asked participants to name dialects of English that they recognised and indicate on a map where these were spoken. The top five dialects recognised were all urban varieties: Scouse (Liverpool), Geordie (Newcastle), Brummie (Birmingham), Cockney (London) and Manc (Manchester). Of these, only Cockney would have been recognised as a variety distinct from the dialects of its hinterland earlier than the nineteenth century. Thus, even as the nineteenth-century dialectologists were bemoaning the fate of rural dialects, new urban varieties were being forged in the crucibles of language and dialect contact that were the towns and cities of the Industrial Revolution. These urban dialects are now presented as being under threat from precisely the same levelling influences that created them in the first place. Trudgill (1999a: 83) presents a map of 'future dialect areas' which would result from these processes of levelling and diffusion which accords very closely with the perceptions of Montgomery's participants. The 'Newcastle' area covers the whole of the North-East, from the Tees to the Tweed; 'Liverpool' stretches from the Ribble estuary to the North Wales coast; and 'London' a huge swathe of the South and South Midlands, and the whole of the south coast from Essex to mid-Dorset. Trudgill's hypothesis is that levelling will lead not to the spread of Standard English/RP, or even to the hegemony of one variety, such as 'Estuary English', but to a number of 'supralocal' varieties, based on the urban varieties of dominant centres, such as Newcastle, Manchester, Birmingham, Norwich, etc. Whilst there is a great deal of evidence for the loss of 'traditional' local accent and/or dialect features and the spread of 'supralocal' variants (see, for instance, Watt 2002 and many of the papers in Foulkes and Docherty 1999), David Britain sounds a note of caution to those who see this as inevitably leading to the 'loss' of dialects. He argues that 'while some dialects are undoubtedly undergoing attrition, new varieties are emerging, driven by both expansion and relocation diffusion, and shaped by contact between local, regional, interregional and other, including standard, varieties'

(2009: 121). In the twenty-first century, just as in the twentieth, the nineteenth, and even in earlier periods, dialects in England are not disappearing so much as changing, albeit perhaps more rapidly than ever before.

1.5 Outline

This book aims to provide an overview of regional variation at all linguistic levels, and of the important issues in research into linguistic variation and change in the dialects of England. Although research being conducted outside of England (in Scotland or the USA, for instance) is referred to where important theoretical and/or methodological issues are raised, the restriction to England (as opposed to Britain or the UK) is necessary because the issues of national, as opposed to regional or local, identity will be more salient in Scotland and Wales. The first three chapters summarise what is known about regional variation in accent, 'grammar' (morphology and syntax) and lexis respectively. Chapter 5 presents an account of research into the processes and results of geographical diffusion and levelling. Chapter 6 deals with issues of identity and indexicality, presenting the results of research which demonstrates that linguistic features can mark identity in different ways for different groups of speakers, and that certain features might become prominent as indexing local identity even as others are 'levelled'.

Exercises

The two extracts below are from the websites of the Northumbrian Language Society (A) and the *Derbyshire Telegraph* (B).

1. Read these extracts and compare them with the extracts from prefaces to nineteenth-century dialect dictionaries on page 4. Consider the following questions and discuss in class:

- What factors are seen as a threat to dialects in the nineteenth-century extracts and in A and B? How are these 'threats' similar in the two different periods and how do they differ?
- Why do you think societies such as the Northumbrian Language Society were set up in the late twentieth century?

2. Enter 'dialect society' into a search engine and look at the home pages of other dialect societies.

- What are the aims of the society?
- Does the home page present the dialect as threatened?

- What effect do you think the society might have on the future of the dialect concerned?

A   The Northumbrian Language Society
Everyone knows at least some of the words of 'The Blaydon Races', that anthem of North-East England, while the sounds of the area's speech are now familiar to many outside the area through such T.V. programmes as 'Auf Wiedersehen, Pet' & 'When the Boat Comes In' and even radio's 'The Archers'. But there's more to the Northumbrian language than 'gannin alang the Scotswood Road' and 'hawway the lads' – this rich, lively and expressive language is inherited directly from the Anglian speech of the Venerable Bede, Saint Cuthbert and, later, Harry Hotspur, with its own ancient and continuing literature. As a means of communication within the Northumbrian community it has survived for one and a half thousand years.

Yet modern influences – greater mobility, compulsory education, national broadcasting networks and contact with other English-speaking countries – are ironing out local differences in speech, and a wealth of vocabulary and characteristic accents are in danger of dying out. National schools' inspectors have acknowledged that a locality's own language is just as valid as any other form of English and should not be deemed 'inferior'. However, the decline in the use of Northumbrian words & pronunciations has been marked over the last century – so, the Northumbrian Language Society was formed in 1983. (www.northumbriana.org.uk/langsoc/about.htm)

B   This is Derbyshire (Derbyshire Telegraph)
If black clouds appeared in the sky and it looked like it was going to rain, how many people would say 'it's guin black over Bill's mother's'?

Or would you tell a girl that you fancied that her smooth skin was 'as lesh as a pig's trough'?

These phrases are probably not heard as often as they used to be in Derbyshire but that has not stopped scores of people sending in examples like these to the Evening Telegraph website following the launch of a new section dedicated to local dialect.

The site has been inundated with feedback from people, notching up 700 hits a week – making it one of the most popular sections.

Visitors to thisisderbyshire.co.uk can send in their favourite words of phrases and hear examples of Derbyshire dialect read by Ted Hancock, who used to give talks on the subject.

'A lot of it is just slang now,' he said.

'Because there are not any works like the pits and engineering, it has died really.'

Former dairy farmer Philip Holland, who has written a book called *Words of the White Peak*, said he was surprised at the interest.

'A lot of the words, like thrompet, meaning a loop to tether a cow on, are not used any more because they are not needed,' he said.

'I remember my father and grandfather saying them and I did a bit until I went to school in the city and then you try to fit in.'

Mr Holland wrote the book on Derbyshire dialects after carrying out research into the subject as part of his English and Creative Writing degree at the University of Derby.

He found that the influence of other dialects and radio and television have all but driven out the broad Derbyshire dialect that has been a feature of the north of the county for centuries. (www. thisisderbyshire.co.uk/dialect/Ey-duck-Derbyshire-dialect-website-proves-popular/article-594338-detail/article.html)

Note

1. See the discussion of this article on John Wells's excellent Estuary English website at www.phon.ucl.ac.uk/home/estuary/glasgow.htm, and, for the true story, Stuart-Smith et al. (2007).

2 Accent variation in England

2.1 Typology of English regional accents

When dividing the country into dialect areas, dialectologists have tended to use mainly phonological criteria. One reason for this is that, whilst educated speakers in England, at least on more formal occasions, tend to use Standard English grammar and vocabulary for the most part, features of regional accent tend to be retained, even though the accents of the well-educated and/or well-travelled may be less 'broad'. As we shall see in Chapter 6, there are factors of solidarity and identity which favour retention of local accent features, but regional syntax and morphology are often viewed as simply 'incorrect' and therefore may be avoided by those who wish to sound educated. For this reason, features of accent provide a much more robust and reliable set of 'clues' than those of dialect to the regional origins of speakers we encounter either face to face or on the telephone. The relative importance of pronunciation in an account of dialectal variation can be seen from the proportion of space devoted to it in Trudgill (1999a): there are sixty-five pages on pronunciation (pp. 20–84), as against twenty-four on grammar (pp. 85–108) and twenty-eight on lexis (pp. 109–36).

Alexander Ellis (1889) divided England into six major dialect areas, on the basis of ten isoglosses (an isogloss is a line drawn on a map marking the division between two areas in which different variants are used). Ellis's divisions are based on four criteria: the pronunciation of words like *some*, the pronunciation of *r*, the pronunciation of the definite article and the pronunciation of words like *house*. All but one of these features are phonological, the 'odd one out' being the reduction of the definite article to [t], [θ] or [ʔ] in his Northern division. Whilst this last criterion does involve phonetic variation, definite article reduction could be considered under the heading of morphology (and will be in this book). Both Wakelin (1983) and Ihalainen (1994) incorporate two further morphological criteria into their classifications, but both of these (finite *be* and periphrastic *do*) serve only to separate dialects of the South-West from those of the rest of England.

More recently, Trudgill has attempted to differentiate the 'traditional' and the 'modern' dialects of England using two sets of phonological criteria. He defines 'traditional dialects' as 'what most people think of when they hear the term **dialect**' and as 'most easily found … in the more remote and peripheral areas of the country' (1999a: 5). The 'traditional dialects' are those which were perceived to be in danger of disappearing when the SED was conducted after World War II, and individual features of these traditional dialects, or rather, accents, are precisely those which have been found to be recessive in the late twentieth and early twenty-first centuries. 'Modern dialects' on the other hand 'represent more recent developments in the English language of England' (1999a: 52), and cannot be differentiated from each other on the basis of the criteria used to distinguish traditional dialects, since many of these have disappeared from 'modern dialects'.

Trudgill provides a checklist of features for 'traditional' and 'modern' dialects, each associated with a keyword which represents a whole set of words in which the same phoneme occurs. His list of 'traditional' dialect features is:

- *long* pronounced /laŋ/ rather than /lɒŋ/
- *night* pronounced /niːt/ rather than /naɪt/
- *blind* pronounced /blɪnd/ rather than /blaɪnd/
- *land* pronounced /lɒnd/ rather than /lænd/
- *arm* pronounced /aːrm/ rather than /aːm/
- *hill* pronounced /ɪl/ rather than /hɪl/
- *seven* pronounced /zevn/ rather than /sevn/
- *bat* pronounced [bat] rather than [bæt]

This list is not intended as an exhaustive account of regional variation in traditional accents, but as a set of binary oppositions whereby any one 'traditional dialect area' can be distinguished any other by at least one feature. Thus Northumberland and the 'Lower North' are only differentiated from each other by *arm* (/aːrm/ in Northumberland, /aːm/ in the Lower North) and *hill* (/hɪl/ in Northumberland, /ɪl/ in the Lower North), and the Western South-West from the Northern South-West only by the use of /zevn/ in the former. Trudgill identifies thirteen dialect areas: Northumberland, Lower North, Lancashire, Staffordshire, South Yorkshire, Lincolnshire, Leicestershire, Western South-West, Northern South-West, Eastern South-West, South-East, Central East and Eastern Counties. These in turn can be placed in larger divisions: there is a major division between 'North' (Scots, Northumberland and

Lower North) and 'South' (everywhere else), and the South is then divided into Central and Southern. The Central area includes the dialects of South Yorkshire, Lancashire and the Midlands, and the South everything south of the Central area.

The traditional dialects as Trudgill describes them here are probably not spoken today throughout the areas he delineates. Some features are more robust than others: /laŋ/ is more likely to be heard in even urban areas of Northumberland than /aːrm/ or /blɪnd/, for instance, and /hɪl/ is certainly still the norm north of the river Wear.[1] The traditional dialects as described by Trudgill are similar to those used by the SED informants and, since these would have been born in the 1880s or earlier, it is not surprising that Trudgill's traditional dialect divisions accord very closely with Ellis's.

A more realistic picture of regional accent differences in England today is provided by Trudgill's account of the pronunciation of 'modern dialects'. As he points out 'many of the features …used … to distinguish between Traditional Dialects cannot be used to discriminate between the Modern Dialects, because they are disappearing from the language and are not found in the speech of the majority of the population' (1999a: 52). The features used to differentiate between modern dialects are:

- *but* pronounced as /bʊt/ or /bʌt/
- *arm* pronounced /aːrm/ or /aːm/
- *singer* pronounced /sɪŋɡə/ or /sɪŋ ə/
- *few* pronounced /fjuː/ or /fuː/
- *coffee* pronounced /kɒfi/ or /kɒfɪ/
- *gate* pronounced /ɡeɪt/ or /ɡeːt/
- *milk* pronounced [mɪʊɫk] or [mɪʊk]

Trudgill provides a useful sentence consisting of words which include these features: *Very few cars made it up the long hill.* (The word *hill* has the advantage over *milk* of being able to differentiate accents in terms of both whether the /h/ is pronounced and whether the final /l/ is vocalised to /ʊ/.) Using these criteria, Trudgill distinguishes sixteen dialect regions, which are in turn placed in larger divisions. The major North/South dividing line has shifted northwards compared to that identified for traditional dialects: 'North' now includes the 'Central' area, i.e. Merseyside and the Midlands, as well as a 'Northern' division consisting of the North-East, the Central North, Central Lancashire and Humberside, whilst the South covers much the same area as it did in Trudgill's map of traditional dialects.

2.2 Trudgill's modern dialect features

2.2.1 But and path: the North–South divide

The main reason for the southward shift of Trudgill's 'Northern' region discussed in the previous section is the inclusion of the feature *but*. Together with another feature not included in Trudgill's list, but discussed later (1999a: 69), the vowel in words such as *path*, this is the most salient marker of 'northern' accents in England today. For both these features, the regionally marked variation is a relatively recent phenomenon, resulting from innovations which started in the South of England in the seventeenth century. The short vowel in words such as *but, flood* and *glove* would have been pronounced /ʊ/, like that in *put, pull*, throughout England in Shakespeare's time, but according to Dobson (1957: 585), there is evidence from c.1640 that the vowel in *cut* was pronounced differently from that of *put*, at least in the South of England. By the middle of the eighteenth century, it was recognised that pronouncing the vowel of *cut* like that of *put* was a northern characteristic. John Kirkby wrote in 1746 that the vowel used by southerners in *cut* was 'scarce known to the inhabitants of the North' and by the end of the eighteenth century the northern pronunciation had become a shibboleth. The famous elocutionist John Walker wrote:

> If the short sound of the letter **u** in *trunk, sunk* etc., differ from the sound of that letter in the northern parts of England, where they sound it like the **u** in *bull*, and nearly as if the words were written *troonk, soonk*, etc., it necessarily follows that every word where that letter occurs must by those provincials be mispronounced. (1791: xiii)

The situation has not changed much between 1791 and the present day: whilst not all speakers from Trudgill's 'Northern' dialect area pronounce words such as *cup* with [ʊ], middle-class speakers in particular tending to use a vowel closer to [ə], very few will make a phonemic distinction between words such as *cup* and *put*. For speakers in this region, pairs of words such as *could* and *cud*; *puss* and *pus*; *put* and *putt* have the same vowel, but in the Southern region the first word in each pair has /ʊ/ and the second has /ʌ/. The distribution of this feature is remarkably stable. Chambers and Trudgill (1998: 106–14), using data from the SED, demonstrate the existence of a 'transition' zone around the Fens, in which speakers do not have consistently 'Northern' or 'Southern' pronunciation, but either have [ʊ] in some words (of the *cup* type) and [ʌ] in others ('mixed') or use a 'compromise' pronunciation [ɤ] ('fudged'). In a later study, David Britain found that younger speakers tended to use what he terms the 'interdialectal' vowel [ɤ] more than older ones, suggesting that this is becoming more common and is 'indicative ... of a stabilization or fossilization of the transition' (2002: 630). So, rather than the 'Southern' feature continuing to spread northwards, the area north of the Fens continues to resist this incursion, and the 'transition' area seems to be developing its own 'interdialectal' variant.

The 'long' vowel in words like *bath, laugh, grass* and *dance* is likewise an innovation of the seventeenth and eighteenth centuries which began in the South. In this case, the new pronunciation probably came from lower-class London speech, as the /ɑ:/ pronunciation was considered 'vulgar' until well into the nineteenth century (see Beal 1999: 107–11 for a full account of this). The distribution of 'short' pronunciations is very similar to that of /ʊ/ in *cup*, etc., discussed above, and equally stable as a marker of 'Northern' pronunciation. Chambers and Trudgill likewise demonstrate the existence of a 'transition' zone in the Fens for this feature, but in this case Britain's later research demonstrates a tendency for younger speakers in the northern part of this area to use [a] more consistently and those in the southern part to use [aː]. In this case, younger speakers are becoming more 'Northern' or 'Southern' in their usage, depending on where within the Fenland region they live. As Britain puts it, there is 'an emerging *isoglossization* of a former transition' (2002: 631).

Certainly, both these features are very salient as markers of 'Northern' vs. 'Southern' speech. The Leeds-born poet Tony Harrison, in his poem 'Them and [ʊz]', in which he describes the way his Yorkshire accent was lampooned by his English teacher at grammar school, focuses on the *cup* vowel, even taking the unusual step of using phonetic notation to make his pronunciation clear. However, the 'flat a', linked with the 'flat cap' of the stereotypical northerner, is also mentioned:

'We say [ʌs] not [ʊz], T.W.!' That shut my trap,
I doffed my flat a's (as in 'flat cap')
(1987: 122)

Wells likewise links these two variants as very strongly associated with 'Northernness', but suggests that the short [a] is the more reliable marker: 'there are many educated northerners who would not be caught dead doing something so vulgar as to pronounce STRUT words with /ʊ/, but who would feel it a denial of their identity as northerners to say BATH words with anything other than short [a]' (1982: 354). (STRUT and BATH here are Wells's keywords standing for the sets of words discussed above.) As the research by Chambers and Trudgill and by Britain discussed above shows, use of a 'compromise' vowel for Wells's STRUT set is a possible strategy for those in a social or geographical 'transition zone', but where BATH is concerned, speakers are more likely to be consistently 'Northern' or 'Southern' in their pronunciation. There are a few lexical exceptions to this rule: in the North-East, the words *master* and *plaster* are pronounced with /ɑː/ by even the broadest dialect speakers, so that *masterclass* has a long vowel in the first half of the compound and a short vowel in the second. A long vowel in *master* can also be heard in other northern locations.[2] Although the use of a short vowel in BATH words is thus a salient and stable feature of 'Northern' accents, the phonemic distinction between /a/ and /ɑː/ is not maintained in South-Western accents. Here, both *bat* and *bath* are pronounced with a lengthened [aˑ] and words such as *hat* and *heart* are distinguished from each other not, as in other English accents, by the length of the vowel, but by the presence of /r/ in *heart*.

2.2.2 Rhoticity

This brings us to the second in Trudgill's list of 'modern dialect' features, one which is also present in his 'traditional' list: the presence or absence of /r/ in words such as *arm*. This feature is very important for the classification and comparison of varieties of English outside England: those in which the orthographic <r> is pronounced /r/ when it occurs before a consonant or word-finally, as in *car, cart, carter*, are termed 'rhotic' whilst those in which it is not are 'non-rhotic'. Rhotic varieties include most North American, Scots and Irish accents, whilst non-rhotic ones include Australian, (most) New Zealand and Welsh accents and the majority of English ones. Historically, the loss of rhoticity in English can be traced back to eighteenth-century London English. John Walker tells us that 'in England, and particularly in London, the *r* in *lard, bard, card, regard*, is pronounced so much in the throat, as to be little more than the middle or Italian *a* lengthened into *baa, baad, caad, regaad*' (1791: 50). However, he makes it clear that he considers this loss of /r/ to be a vulgarism and not to be recommended to the readers of his dictionary, who were aiming at a 'correct' pronunciation. He goes on to contrast the 'rough' Irish pronunciation of /r/ with the 'softer' English variety, and concludes: 'if this letter is too forcibly pronounced in Ireland, it is often too feebly pronounced in England, and particularly in London, where it is sometimes entirely sunk' (1791: 50).

Throughout most of the nineteenth century, non-rhotic pronunciations continued to be condemned, but by the time Daniel Jones's pronouncing dictionary was published in 1917, non-rhotic pronunciations had become characteristic of RP.[3] The spread of non-rhotic pronunciation can thus be seen as a change 'from below', beginning in non-standard London English and spreading geographically northwards and socially 'upwards' until, in the early twenty-first century, it is the rhotic pronunciations that are marked as non-standard in England. Even within rhotic areas there is evidence that younger people are less likely to pronounce /r/ in words such as *arm*. In other words, rhoticity is a recessive feature in England.

A comparison of Trudgill's map 5, showing the distribution of rhoticity in traditional dialects (1999a: 27), with his map 12 (1999a: 55), showing the same distribution in modern dialects, reveals the 'shrinkage' which has taken place. In the 'traditional' map, rhotic accents are marked across a huge swathe south and west of a line running from Kent to the West Midlands, skirting the conurbations of London, Birmingham and Wolverhampton, but including Oxford; most of the North-West from Chester to the Lake District; and everywhere to the north of a line running from just south of Durham to Carlisle. In the 'modern' dialect map, the last of these has disappeared completely, the North-Western area has shrunk to a small Lancastrian enclave with Blackburn at its centre, and even the Southern stronghold has shifted westwards, so that the far South-East from Kent to Portsmouth is now excluded. In England, rhoticity is now very much a Western, and primarily a South-Western, feature. Although, as Britain (2009: 130) points out, there has been no recent nationwide survey of rhoticity, studies of individual locations in the 'rhotic' South-West by Dudman (2000), Jones (1998) and Williams (1991) provide evidence for the loss of this feature. Interestingly, the degree of loss seems to increase as we move eastwards: Dudman's study of St Ives in Cornwall found that younger people, whilst using rhotic pronunciations half as frequently as elderly speakers, still had a rhoticity level of 25 per cent; Jones's investigation in East Devon and West Somerset found some rhoticity amongst younger speakers; but Williams's research on the Isle of Wight revealed a total loss of rhoticity amongst younger speakers.

In Lancashire, at least within the area marked as rhotic on Trudgill's 'modern dialect' map, rhoticity seems a little more robust: Vivian's (2000) study of speakers from Accrington, Burnley and Blackburn found that, whilst some loss was evident, younger speakers still had high levels of rhoticity, especially in Accrington and Blackburn. Within the Lancashire area, rhoticity is locally very salient, as it differentiates the dialects of towns such as Blackburn and Accrington from that of the city of Manchester. As we shall see in Chapter 6, features which appear to be receding on a national level may still be very important markers of local identity within specific regions.

2.2.3 'Velar nasal plus'

The next keyword in Trudgill's list of 'modern' dialect features is *singer*, pronounced /sɪŋɡə/ or /sɪŋə/. The variable concerned here is what Wells (1982: 365) calls 'velar nasal plus': the tendency for speakers in the North-West and West Midlands to pronounce the orthographic <g> in the cluster <ng> when elsewhere in England only a velar nasal /ŋ/ is pronounced. For speakers with 'velar nasal plus', the velar nasal is not a separate phoneme, but a variant of /n/ which only and always occurs before /ɡ/ or /k/, but for those without this feature, *sin: sing; win: wing; thin: thing*, etc., are 'minimal pairs', words differentiated by a single phoneme, and the words *singer* /sɪŋə/ and *finger* /fɪŋɡə/ do not strictly rhyme.[4] According to Trudgill (1999a: 59), the area in which 'velar nasal plus' is found stretches from Birmingham to Blackburn, west of the Pennines, and thus includes Birmingham, Liverpool, Manchester and Derby (but not Nottingham), and, as such, differentiates the accents of the West Midlands from those of the East Midlands.

The geographical distribution of this feature, in an (admittedly large) enclave, would suggest that it is a 'relic' of a formerly more widespread pronunciation, and such is the case. According to Dobson (1957: 963–5), the first clear evidence for 'loss of [ɡ] after [ŋ]' does not appear until the seventeenth century, and most eighteenth-century authors who describe English pronunciation fail to provide a separate notation for the velar nasal. Within the North-West and West Midlands, this feature is very stable and not at all stigmatised. This may be because, since the late eighteenth century, attention has been focused on the phenomenon which is often inaccurately described as 'dropping the <g>' in word-final *-ing*. In fact, in RP and all accents except those with 'velar nasal plus', there is no /ɡ/ to drop, the stigmatised pronunciation being one in which the alveolar nasal /n/ is used instead of the velar /ŋ/. Such is the power of spelling to influence our notions of 'correct' pronunciation. In the North-West and West Midlands, pronunciations such as [sɪŋɡɪŋ] for *singing* are considered 'correct' or even 'posh', compared to [sɪŋɡɪn].

2.2.4 'Yod-dropping'

The next feature in Trudgill's list is, like 'velar nasal plus', confined to a very specific area, but this time in the East rather than the West. Words such as *few* are pronounced with a glide /j/ (known as 'yod') followed by a vowel everywhere except in East Anglia, where pronunciations such as /fuː/ are heard. This has come to be recognised as a stereotypical East Anglian feature: the Turkey farmer Bernard Matthews famously advertises his product as 'bootiful'. Although the restriction of 'yod-dropping' to an enclave and the geographical isolation of East Anglia might suggest that this, like rhoticity and 'velar nasal plus', is a relic feature, it is, in fact an extension of an innovation which affects most varieties of English to a greater or lesser extent. Until the seventeenth century, the /j/ was pronounced in words such as *chew, rude* and *blue,* but it began to be assimilated into the palatal consonant /tʃ/ in *chew* and dropped from *rude, blue,* etc. This was a very gradual process, and yod-dropping was considered incorrect for a long time. The Scottish elocutionist James Elphinston states in 1787 that it is 'vulgar indolence or bluntness' to 'sink the liquefaction' in *peruse, rule,* making them *per-ooz, rool,* and pronunciations such as /bljuː/ for *blue* and /sjuːt/ for *suit* persist well into the twentieth century in conservative RP. In most varieties within England, including RP, yod-dropping is now found in words such as *chew, rude* and *suit;* after /n/, /t/ and /d/ in words such as *new, tune* and *due,* it is found in London and parts of the Midlands; but the full extension of yod-dropping to all environments, including words such as *beautiful, few* and *human,* is largely confined to East Anglia.

2.2.5 'happY tensing'

The distribution of Trudgill's next feature, the final vowel in *coffee,* is much less straightforward. The feature referred to by Wells (1982: 257) as '*happ*Y tensing', i.e. the pronunciation of this vowel as a tense and sometimes long /i(ː)/ rather than a short, lax /ɪ/ or even /ɛ/, is, according to Trudgill, found everywhere in England except 'the Central North, Central Lancashire, Northwest Midlands and Central Midlands' (1999a: 62). Thus, the area in which '*happ*Y tensing' does not occur seems fairly coherent. However, if we look at the areas in which it does occur, the distribution is strange: the whole of the South has this feature, but it is also found in three coastal enclaves in the North: the areas around Liverpool, Hull and the North-East coast from the Tees to the Tweed. Within these northern areas, '*happ*Y tensing' is very salient: it differentiates the accent of Liverpool from those of Manchester and other Lancashire towns, that of Hull from other Yorkshire towns and cities, and those of Newcastle, Sunderland and Durham from those of Carlisle to the west and North Yorkshire to the south.[5] Both Wells (1982) and Trudgill (1999a) describe '*happ*Y tensing' as a relatively recent innovation, and Trudgill suggests that it is spreading from south to north:

> The 'ee' vowel in *very* is obviously spreading rather rapidly. Most Traditional Dialects in England, except in the far south, have (or had)

short 'i' /ɪ/ in *very* ... This has now been replaced in most of the South
and Midlands by 'veree' /veriː/, which seems to be spreading northwards quite quickly. It has already, as we have seen, 'jumped' over the
intervening areas to the urban centres of Liverpool and Newcastle.
(1999a: 82)

I have argued, however, that this feature is 'neither so recent, nor so
southern as has been assumed' (2000: 494), since there is evidence for
'*happ*Y tensing' in pronouncing dictionaries of the eighteenth century
written in both London and Newcastle, as well as dialectal evidence
from nineteenth- and early twentieth-century Northumberland. It may
well be the case that '*happ*Y tensing' is spreading in the early twenty-first
century, but, rather than this being a simple South-to-North movement,
it would appear to be diffusing from the urban centres of Liverpool and
Tyneside as well. Increasingly, though, a tense vowel in words like *happy*
is perceived as the norm in England, and those accents with a lax vowel
are marked. In every case, it is the lax variant which is stigmatised.

2.2.6 Monophthongal versus diphthongal made

The pronunciation of words such as *gate* and *made* is described by
Trudgill (1999a: 62) as involving a contrast between a monophthongal
/eː/ and a diphthong /eɪ/, with the latter pronunciation found, with the
exception of the far South-West, everywhere south of a line which runs
below Sheffield, but above Liverpool and Manchester, and the monophthong everywhere to the north of this line. The diphthongisation is a
fairly recent innovation, first noticed by Thomas Batchelor in 1809, and
has probably spread northwards and westwards since then. However,
traditional accents in the far North-East, especially those of Tyneside,
have a centring diphthong /eə/ or even /ɪə/ rather than a monophthong,
so the 'North' is not as homogeneous as Trudgill's account would
suggest. Indeed, as we shall see in Chapter 5, there is evidence that, in the
Tyneside area, it is the monophthongal variant that is spreading at the
expense of the traditional centring diphthong. Watt and Milroy (1999)
found that, in a study of speech recorded in 1994, only the older,
working-class males used /ɪə/ in the majority of tokens of what Wells
(1982) classifies as FACE vowels. Amongst all other groups, the most
frequent variant was /eː/, with /eɪ/ emerging as a minority variant in the
speech of some young, middle-class males and females. Watt and Milroy
suggest that the younger Tynesiders are signalling that they do not wish
to identify with the 'old-fashioned' cloth-cap-and-clogs image of their
fathers, but still wish to be identified as northerners, so they are assimi-

lating their speech to a pan-Northern norm. On the other hand, on the southern boundary of Trudgill's 'geht' region, the diphthongal variant is spreading from urban centres such as Liverpool and Manchester, and the traditional Lancashire monophthong is associated with more 'old-fashioned' speech. This demonstrates again that variant pronunciations have local values assigned to them by speakers, a point to which we will return in Chapter 6.

2.2.7 /l/-vocalisation

The last keyword in Trudgill's list of 'modern' dialect features is *milk*. Here, the variant which is of interest is the 'vocalisation' of /l/, so that *milk* is pronounced /mɪʊk/. This affects all words in which /l/ appears after a vowel, so *tell, doll, call, full* would all have diphthongs rather than a vowel followed by /l/. This appears to be a very recent development in London English: according to Wells (1982: 259), it is first described by Daniel Jones in 1909 as a feature of 'London dialectal speech'. It has now spread geographically throughout the South-East of England, and socially into 'Estuary English' and even RP. Both Wells and Trudgill predict that /l/-vocalisation will become the norm in England in the same way that loss of rhoticity has. However, this may not spread throughout the country, because /l/-vocalisation depends on the presence of a more 'vowel-like' variant of /l/, known as 'dark /l/' and represented in the International Phonetic Alphabet (IPA) as [ɫ]. In RP and most accents of England, this is found after vowels and contrasts with the 'clear' [l] found before vowels: thus *lilt* would be pronounced [lɪɫt] but *lilly* [lɪli]. However, in the North-East of England (as in Wales), this clear/dark distinction is not maintained, and a clear [l] can be used in all positions, so *milk* would be pronounced [mɪlk]. Where /l/ is followed by a nasal /m/ or /n/ a vowel /ə/ is inserted between the two consonants, as a clear [l] followed immediately by /m/ or /n/ is very difficult to produce. Thus the Northumbrian river *Aln* and the town at its estuary *Alnmouth* are pronounced [alən, alənmauθ]. Britain (2009: 140) confirms that 'the advance of the vocalisation of /l/ is blocked or con-siderably decelerated by the absence of a clear–dark /l/ distinction, and it is notable that those areas which have or have had until recently a clear /l/ in both onset and coda resist /l/ vocalisation'. So, this feature may not become as ubiquitous as Wells and Trudgill predicted, but, in areas where the clear/dark contrast is maintained, there is evidence of /l/-vocalisation spreading as far north as Derby (Docherty and Foulkes 1999). We will consider further the geographical diffusion of 'Estuary English' features such as this in Chapter 5.

2.2.8 'H Dropping'

Trudgill's test sentence uses the word *hill* as a diagnostic of /l/-vocalis-ation, but this keyword does double duty, as it also has initial <h>. The distribution of 'H Dropping' in accents of England is perhaps more of a social than a geographical phenomenon: since the late eighteenth century, failure to pronounce initial /h/ in all but a very restricted set of French- or Latin-derived words (*honour, hour* and related words) has become highly stigmatised, so that it is now, according to Wells, 'the single most powerful pronunciation shibboleth in England' (1982: 254). However, whilst 'H Dropping' is marked socially, it is the norm geographically, and H Retaining areas are isolated. Trudgill's map 6 is discussed under the heading of 'traditional' dialects, and shows H Retention in 'two geographically peripheral parts of the country, the northeast and East Anglia' (1999a: 29). In East Anglia, H Retention is now recessive: according to Hughes et al. (2005: 79) it is still found in 'rural East Anglia' but 'has been partly lost in Norwich'. Despite the fact that it is stigmatised, H Dropping appears to be spreading rather than receding. The last area of resistance seems to be the North-East, where H Retention is still common from Sunderland northwards, though recent research does suggest that some H Dropping is found even here. Within the North-east, H Dropping distinguishes the accent of Teesside from that of Tyneside, with those of Wearside and County Durham demonstrating some H Dropping (Burbano-Elizondo 2008).

2.3 Summary: Trudgill's 'modern' dialect features and beyond

Table 2.1 represents the distribution of the features discussed above as a set of binary oppositions, according to which each regional accent of England differs from any other with regard to at least one feature.

As I have indicated in the discussion above, Table 2.1 does not provide a foolproof method of distinguishing every English regional accent, but it does present a workable typology. The North-East and Humberside are geographically contiguous, and are distinguished from each other only with respect to the retention of /h/ in the North-East. Those who are familiar with the accent of Humberside, and particularly the city of Kingston upon Hull, will know that there are other features which are diagnostic of the local accent: the fronting of the vowel in words such as *goat* to [øː] and the pronunciation of words such as *early* as /ɛːliː/. Both these features are very well known in the area: in humorous texts, the people of Hull are described as making *fern curls*, and the nickname of Hull F.C. Rugby League team is the 'Airlie Birds' (/ɛːliː bɜːdz/). In fact,

Table 2.1 Features of 'modern' English dialects (after Hughes et al. 2005: 71).

	/ʌ/ in but	/ɑː/ in bath	/r/ in arm	[ŋg] in sting	/j/ in few	/iː/ in coffee	/eɪ/ in gate	/l/- vocalisation	/h/ in hill
North-East	x	x	x	x	✓	✓	x	x	✓
Humberside	x	x	x	x	✓	✓	x	x	x
Central North	x	x	x	x	✓	x	x	x	x
Central Lancs.	x	x	✓	✓	✓	x	x	x	x
Merseyside	x	x	x	✓	✓	✓	✓	x	x
N-W Midlands	x	x	x	✓	✓	x	✓	x	x
W Midlands	x	x	x	✓	✓	✓	✓	x	x
E Midlands	x	x	x	x	x	x	✓	x	x
S Midlands	✓	✓	x	x	x	✓	✓	x	x
East Anglia	✓	✓	x	x	x	✓	✓	x	✓
South-East	✓	✓	x	x	✓	✓	✓	✓	x
E South-West	✓	x	✓	x	✓	✓	✓	x	x
W South-West	✓	x	✓	x	✓	✓	x	x	x

the fronted vowel in *goat* is increasingly found elsewhere in Yorkshire and the /ɛːliː/ pronunciation is also typical of Teesside, but the combination of the two keeps the accent of Hull distinct from those of both its nearest neighbours. Teesside belongs typologically, as well as geographically, between the North-East and Humberside, as the Teesside accent does not retain /h/ (Hughes et al. 2005: 70).

According to Table 2.1, the accents of Merseyside and the West Midlands are typologically identical, and that of the North-West Midlands differs from these only with respect to the lack of 'happY tensing'. (In fact, the accents of some of the cities included in the North-West Midlands area by Hughes et al., notably Chester, probably do have this feature now, under the influence of Liverpool.) Again, these areas are geographically close, if not contiguous, and the similarities between the accents are to be expected, but there are also distinguishing features not included in Table 2.1. The accent of Merseyside, especially in its broad 'Scouse' version, is distinguished by the presence of affricated or fricated consonants where other accents have /p, t, k/. Thus *rap* is pronounced [rapf] or even [raɸ], *rat* [rats] or [ras] and *rack* [rakx] or [rax]. Apart from the areas of the North-West Midlands influenced by Liverpool (which should perhaps be reassigned to Merseyside), this is not found in any other accent within England. Elsewhere, these consonants are tending to become glottalised or replaced by glottal stops, a phenomenon to which we will return in Chapter 5.

If we look at the lower end of Table 2.1, we see that the South Midlands is differentiated from East Anglia by one feature: the retention of /h/ in the latter area. Since, as we have seen, this feature is recessive in East Anglia, the accents of these two areas will become more similar. It is probably not surprising that the East South-West and the West South-West are differentiated from each other by just one feature: the presence of a diphthongal pronunciation of words such as *gate* in the former. The area which seems to have no close match with any other here is the East Midlands. This would appear to suggest that the accent of this area is very distinctive, but the evidence from perceptual studies such as Montgomery (2006) seems to indicate the opposite, namely that there is very little sense of what an East Midlands accent is.

In this chapter, I have attempted to present a 'broad-brush' account of accent variation within England, with some attention to the historical origins of variation and the findings of more recent research on the development of these accents. As I have indicated in the last section, individual accents are often distinguished from those of neighbouring areas by features which are not included in this 'broad-brush' typology, and local residents are often keenly aware of what might seem to an outsider to be trivial differences, sometimes involving the pronunciation of individual words. As linguists, we are interested in typological patterns and the questions these might generate. Do similarities and differences reflect historical settlement patterns? Might the presence or absence of one linguistic feature in a region 'block' the adoption of an innovatory pattern which is spreading elsewhere? As sociolinguists, we might also be interested in the ways in which these differences in pronunciation continue to express and preserve local and regional identity in the face of globalisation. These questions will be explored in later chapters, but differences between the linguistic outputs of speakers from different geographical areas are not confined to those which involve pronunciation (or accent): differences of dialect are also important, so, before going on to discuss theoretical issues, I shall outline the main distinctions between dialects of England with respect to grammar (Chapter 3) and vocabulary (Chapter 4).

Exercises

The British Library's 'Sounds Familiar' website has a range of very useful resources for the study of accents. One feature is 'your voices', where students from schools and colleges throughout the UK have sent in recordings of themselves reading the children's story *Mr Tickle*.

You can find this website at www.bl.uk/learning/langlit/sounds/your-voices/. From the interactive map, listen to at least two recordings from different parts of the country.

- Using Table 2.1 as a template, produce a table showing which of Trudgill's 'modern' dialect features are used by each speaker. (Note: the exact words used by Trudgill as examples do not all appear in *Mr Tickle*, so you need to find equivalents. *Very, made, up* and *long* are in the text, but for *few*, listen to *duty*; for *cars*, listen to *arms*; for *hill*, listen to *house* for /h/ and *small* for /l/.)
- What other features of accent do you notice in these readings? (The 'analyse your accent' section on the website will help you with this.)
- You may want to make a recording of yourself or a friend reading *Mr Tickle* and submit it to the website. Full instructions are provided.

Further reading

Volume 1 of Wells (1982) provides an account of the keywords used in this chapter, along with a survey of the major variables in accents of English. Volume 2 provides a more detailed description of accent variation in British English, and a more recent account can be found in Kortmann and Upton (2008). Hughes et al. (2005) provides a typology of accent variation in the British Isles and a more detailed account of a limited range of accents. Foulkes and Docherty (1999) is a collection of papers on specific accents of British and Irish English, each of which includes a description of the phonology of the accent concerned and a study of variation and change.

Notes

1. Both these features can be heard in the extracts from the Tyneside Linguistic Survey in the Newcastle Electronic Corpus of Tyneside English (NECTE). One speaker (GE052), aged 45 when recorded in 1969, says 'maybe a little bit longer' (/laŋə/) and 'but then I come over here' (/hiːɐ/).
2. For an explanation of this phenomenon, which has nothing to do with influence from southern varieties or RP, see Beal (1985).
3. See Beal (1999: 163–71) and Mugglestone (1995: 98–103) for a full account of this.
4. As a speaker of 'velar nasal plus', I could not understand why, when I went to university, people found my pronunciation of words such as *sing* amusing. As far as I was concerned, there was a <g> there, and I was pronouncing it correctly. A course in phonetics enlightened me, but did not change my pronunciation.
5. In fact, the area around Hull appears not so much as an enclave as a continuation of the 'Eastern' area of '*happ*Y tensing' northwards from Lincolnshire.

3 Dialect variation in England: morphology and syntax

3.1 Introduction: the study of regional grammar

In the previous chapter, we saw that typologies of English dialects have tended to be constructed according to phonological criteria: strictly speaking, they are typologies of accents rather than dialects. Comparing the classificatory criteria of Ellis (1889), Wakelin (1983) and Trudgill (1990), Ihalainen (1994) found that, out of nineteen criteria, only three could be considered morphological or syntactic: the use of *t'* or *th'* for *the*, the use of finite *be* and the use of periphrastic *do*; and of these, the first is used only by Ellis and the latter two only by Wakelin (and then only to separate the South-West from the rest of England). Ihalainen himself adds another feature, 'pronoun exchange', which involves what would be the subject form in Standard English being used in object position and vice versa, as in *Her said to I.* Ihalainen claims that this 'is one of the few features that divide the country up in an east–west direction' (1994: 231). However, as we shall see in Section 3.4.3, this feature is also found, albeit to a limited extent, in the North-East of England and in East Anglia, so it cannot be seen as a 'western' characteristic.

Kortmann's comparative study of the morphosyntactic characteristics of British English varieties identifies a 'north–south divide ... with the core of the north constituted by Sc[ottish]E[nglish], Orkney/Shetland and the dialects of North England, and the south constituted by the Southwest, the Southeast and East Anglia' (2008: 490). Kortmann is silent on the place of Midlands dialects here because these are not covered in the volume, but what is notable is the persistence of a 'Northumbrian/Southumbrian' divide which can be traced back to Anglo-Saxon times, when the Anglian dialect of Northumbria was spoken from the Humber to the Forth. Having said that, some of the features identified as 'Northern' by Kortmann, such as the use of special second person plural forms, e.g. *youse*, are innovative rather than conservative. Kortmann's lists of distinctively 'Northern' and 'Southern' features are reproduced below:

'Northern' features

- special forms or phrases for the second person plural pronoun
- wider range of uses of the progressive (e.g. *I'm liking this. What are you wanting?*)
- *be* as perfect auxiliary (e.g. *They're not left school yet*)
- double modals (e.g. *I tell you what we might should do*)
- epistemic *mustn't* (= 'can't, it is concluded that … not', e.g. *This mustn't be true*)
- resumptive/shadow pronouns (e.g. *This is the house which I painted it yesterday*)
- lack of inversion/lack of auxiliaries in *wh*-questions (e.g. *What you doing?*)
- lack of inversion in main clause *yes/no* questions (e.g. *You get the point?*)

'Southern' features

- *a*-prefixing on *-ing* forms (e.g. *They wasn't a-doin' nothin' wrong*)
- *ain't* as the negated form of *be* (e.g. *They're all in there, ain't they*)
- *ain't* as the negated form of *have* (e.g. *I ain't had a look at them yet*)
- invariant non-concord tags (e.g. *innit/in't it/isn't it* in *They had them in their hair, innit?*)
- relative particle *what* (e.g. *This is the man what painted my house*)

Not all of the features identified as 'Northern' here are found throughout the North of England. For instance, as we shall see in Section 3.3.8, double modals are extremely rare in England, and confined to restricted and recessive use in Tyneside and Northumberland. On the other hand, relative particle *what* is, as we shall see in Section 3.4.5, found in the 'lower North' much more than in the far North. With regard to both these features, the dialects of the far North pattern with those of Scotland, which is not surprising given the geographical closeness and contiguity between the two areas. Kortmann admits that his comparative analysis 'is necessarily subject to severe constraints regarding the breadth and depth of coverage' and, as such, 'may give the impression of a much higher degree of homogeneity and pervasiveness than is appropriate' (2008: 478). Nevertheless, it is interesting that, just as we saw in Section 2.2.1 that the North/South division marked by the BATH and STRUT isoglosses is stable and robust, this is also the clearest division with regard to morphosyntactic features.

Much research into English varieties, both that conducted within the framework of traditional dialectology and the more recent studies of variation and change, such as those in Foulkes and Docherty (1999), has tended to focus on phonological and phonetic variation, so much so that a whole new discipline of 'sociophonetics' has been created (Foulkes 2005). Nevertheless, morphological and syntactic variation has not been entirely neglected. Jenny Cheshire was one of the pioneers: her (1982) study of the language of teenagers in Reading focused on morphological variation such as that between *did* and *done* in e.g. *We done our homework.* Trudgill and Chambers (1991) and Milroy and Milroy (1993) edited collections of studies in grammatical (morphological and syntactic) variation. The publication of these two volumes edited by established scholars in the fields of sociolinguistics and dialectology heralded an upsurge of interest in regional grammar within England. This was taken up by e.g. Anderwald (2002), Beal and Corrigan (2000, 2002, 2005a, 2005b, 2007), Britain (2001, 2002), Tagliamonte and Ito (2002), Tagliamonte and Lawrence (2000), Tagliamonte and Smith (2002, 2005, 2006), Tagliamonte et al. (2005) and Hermann et al. (2008).[1] Indeed Cornips and Corrigan have recently (2005) set out the case for a subdiscipline of 'socio-syntax' analogous to the now-established sociophonetics.

The study of morphological and syntactic variation does present the researcher with a number of problems. Although there has been much discussion of the 'observer's paradox'[2] and the difficulty of collecting 'natural' data, it is at least relatively easy to collect enough tokens of phonological and phonetic variants, since they are likely to occur within even a short stretch of speech. However, many of the morphological and syntactic features which display regional and social variation are restricted to specific pragmatic contexts, and so can prove elusive. For instance, it is very difficult to elicit tokens of interrogative structures from an interview in which it is the researcher who asks the questions. As Anderwald and Wagner (2007) point out, data collected from oral history interviews, or even anecdotes, tend to be in the past tense, making it difficult to find tokens of constructions referring to future time. For this reason questionnaires have often been used to determine whether speakers use and/or are aware of morphological and syntactic variants. This was the technique used in the SED, where informants would be asked to supply the form that they would use in a particular sentence. For instance, to elicit the use of different forms of possessive relative pronoun (Standard English *whose*), informants were asked to 'complete' the sentence: *That's the chap … uncle drowned.* This resulted in a wide range of variants throughout the country, as we shall see when relative pronouns are discussed further in Section 3.4.5 below. In their 1989 survey of British dialect grammar, Cheshire and Edwards used a questionnaire designed to be 'child-friendly' and to be used in the context of class discussion in schools around the country. Using cartoons and section headings which were often amusing or diverting, they presented sets of sentences incorporating features of non-standard morphology and syntax along with boxes for the groups to tick if the sentence-types were used in their area. For instance, a section dealing with variation in present tense verb endings is headed 'Got a sweet tooth?' and illustrated with a cartoon of a child eating sweets. The sentences in this section are:

12. ☐ I **likes** toffees
13. ☐ We **liken** toffees
14. ☐ We **likes** toffees
15. ☐ Thee **likes** toffees
16. ☐ Thee **like** toffees
17 ☐ She **like** toffees

(Cheshire et al. 1993: 88)

By using questionnaires, both the SED and the Survey of British Dialect Grammar were able to obtain comparative information from across the whole country. However, there are drawbacks to this method. As I suggested in Section 2.1, regional or non-standard morphology and syntax are often regarded as 'incorrect' or 'bad grammar', so there is a risk that informants might deny using these features or give 'standard' responses. On the other hand, exposure to a range of dialects through the media, especially in soap operas such as *EastEnders* (London), *Coronation Street* (Manchester) and *Emmerdale* (Yorkshire), could have the opposite effect, as informants might claim familiarity with features heard on TV rather than in their own locality.

The alternative to using questionnaires is to collect a large body of data, either from informal linguistic interviews, or from recordings made for other purposes, such as oral history, and search the texts for tokens of the variables which are of interest. Until recently, this approach has tended to be used in studies of variation within individual localities, such as Cheshire's (1982) study of Reading. The advent of digital recording and search tools has made it possible for researchers to find examples in large bodies of text, or corpora, and for comparisons to be made across material recorded in different places. The papers by Tagliamonte and various co-authors cited above are all studies based on comparison of data from a range of localities in England, Scotland and Northern Ireland. These data were collected systematically, using the same methodology and sample design, so that such comparisons would be valid. The studies by Anderwald and Wagner et al. are based on data from the British National Corpus (BNC) and the Freiburg Regional English Dialects (FRED) corpus. The latter was compiled from oral history data held in archives within and beyond the UK, again in order to facilitate comparisons. Beal and Corrigan (2005a) compare results from two corpora compiled from interviews carried out in Tyneside and Sheffield.

As we shall see, the findings of these corpus-based studies sometimes contradict those of questionnaire-based research, and often reveal nuances of variation that had not hitherto been discovered. However, as Cheshire (2005) points out, there is a danger that corpus-based studies will divert attention from the study of constructions which do not occur frequently enough for sufficient tokens to be found even in large bodies of data. If we are to gain a complete picture of variation across regional dialects, then a combination of corpus and questionnaire methodologies will have to be used.

3.2 Regional, non-standard or sub-standard?

As I have pointed out in Section 3.1, regional and other non-standard forms and constructions are often viewed by non-linguists as being 'uneducated', 'incorrect' or simply 'bad grammar'. Whilst attitudes to regional accents tend to be ambivalent, with positive and negative traits attributed to them and their speakers, non-standard morphology and syntax are rarely seen in a positive light. One reason for this could be that, whereas at least some regional accents are fairly well recognised, and dialect vocabulary is often considered 'authentic', many features of non-standard morphology and syntax are fairly widespread within England, and so are considered to be social rather than regional variables. Of course, as Cheshire and Milroy point out, there is an important difference between *non-standard* and *sub-standard*:

> The term *standardization* can be used of phenomena outside language and means the imposition of uniformity upon a class of objects. Thus, we may describe a set of motor-car components, or electric plugs, or a coinage system, as being 'standardized'. When such objects are described as 'sub-standard', the implication is that they are not of the quality required to perform their function in the most reliable way ... When, on the other hand, we speak of items as *non-standard*, there is no such value-judgement. The best analogy here is with hand-made, as against factory, tools. Whereas factories produce large numbers of items (e.g. spades) that are all identical, those made by traditional craftsmen are all slightly different. (1993: 3–4)

Some features of non-standard morphology and syntax actually function rather better than their Standard English equivalents. For instance, where Standard English fails to differentiate singular from plural second person pronouns, using *you/your* whether one person or more are being addressed, regional dialects employ a range of variants, from the traditional singular *thee*/*thy* of some Northern dialects to the plural *yous* of urban dialects such as those of Liverpool and Newcastle, and the East Anglian *you … together*. Even widespread and highly stigmatised variants such as the use of *done* as the past tense form of *do*, as in the football managers' cliché *The boy done good*, is, as demonstrated by Cheshire (1982), used in a systematic and rule-based way, differentiating past tense uses of the lexical verb from the auxiliary *do*. Thus, the football manager might say *The boy done good, didn't he?*, with *done* as the past tense form of the lexical verb and *did* the auxiliary.

In fact, corpus-based studies have discovered that some of these 'non-standard' constructions do show regional variation. For instance, Anderwald found that 'negative concord, widely held to show no regional, only social differentiation across the English-speaking world … is still considerably rarer in non-standard language today in the North [of England] than in the South' (2005: 134). Cheshire et al. had been surprised to find that children in the North were less likely to tick the box containing the sentence *I won't do nothing silly*, but they speculated that this was due to the construction being 'so heavily stigmatized that despite our best efforts to raise the status of dialect in the classroom, pupils simply fail to report it' (1993: 76). This, of course, begs the question of why northerners should feel more 'ashamed' than southerners. Anderwald's study demonstrates that shame is not the issue here: the construction is genuinely rarer in the North, a finding confirmed in Beal and Corrigan's (2005b) corpus-based study of negation in Tyneside English.[3] The lesson we can take from this is not to dismiss as uninteresting constructions which have previously been considered 'non-standard' rather than regional. There is much work to be done before we have a full picture of regional variation in morphology and syntax, but in the following sections, I shall attempt to summarise the state of our knowledge and point out interesting areas for future research.

3.3 Variation in the verb phrase

3.3.1 *Past tense paradigms*

Even in Standard English, there is a good deal of irregularity and even variability in the morphological patterns of verbs, particularly with regard to the past tense and past participle. Whereas 'regular' or 'weak' verbs have the ending *-ed* in both of these (*walk*/*walked*/*walked*), those variously referred to as 'irregular' or 'strong' verbs display a wide range of patterns. Some have the same form for present, past and past participle (*put/put/put*), others have a different vowel in each (*swim/swam/swum*), or one vowel in the present and another which is used in both the past and participle (*hang/hung/hung*), or the same in the present and participle and a different one in the past (*run/ran/run*). In addition to changes in the vowel (known as *ablaut*), some have an *-n* ending in the past participle, e.g. *freeze/froze/frozen; tear/tore/torn*, and others have *-t* rather than *-d* in both spelling and pronunciation, such as *bend/bent/bent*.[4]

When we look at past tense and participle forms in regional dialects, the picture becomes even more complicated. The range of available patterns is the same, but verbs are distributed differently. Anderwald (2009) has examined the FRED corpus in an attempt both to determine the range and distribution of paradigms across regional dialects, and to discover whether the kind of 'supra-regional' features identified in socio-phonetic studies such as those of Foulkes and Docherty (1999) can also be identified in morphology. Anderwald finds that what she calls 'weaki-fication', i.e. the use of a regular or 'weak' paradigm where Standard English has a 'strong' one, is comparatively rare, unless we count examples with a *-t* suffix, such as *tellt, sellt*, which tend to be found in Northern (and, for that matter, Scottish) dialects. She also finds that there is no regional patterning to the distribution of non-standard strong verb forms. Much more common is the tendency to reduce 'strong' paradigms with three contrasting forms in Standard English (*drink/drank/drunk*) to two (*drink/drunk/drunk*) and those with two (*come/came/come*) to one (*come/come/come*). She also notes a strong tendency for 'ablaut' forms to be levelled to orthographic <u> and/or phonological /ʊ~ʌ/ as in the examples above. However, evidence from the NECTE corpus (Beal 2008: 375) suggests that, in the North-East, many of these are levelled to <a>, as in *drink/drank/drank; ring/rang/rang; sing/sang/sang; swim/swam/swam*.

As far as regional variation goes, Anderwald confirms that forms such as *tellt, sellt* are found in the North, finds that past tense *eat* tends to be found in the South-West, and finds that a small group of verbs with level-ling to /ʊ/~/ʌ/ (*do/done/done; come/come/come; run/run/run*) are very common in the South-East. This tallies with the results of the Survey of British Dialect Grammar that past tense *done* was reported with a frequency of 92 per cent in the South, as against 67 per cent in the Midlands and 60.5 per cent in the North (Cheshire et al. 1993: 78). Anderwald, like Cheshire et al. notes that forms such as *done* are precisely those identified by Bybee and Moder (1983) as conforming to the 'preferred schema for past tense forms in English' (Cheshire et al. 1993: 78). Anderwald suggests that these are the forms most likely to spread in the process of supra-localisation. However, before we can be confident that these forms are spreading from the South-East, more research needs to be done on their relative frequency in areas outside the South-East at different times and/or in the speech of different generations.

3.3.2 Present tense verb endings

In Standard English, the paradigm of the present tense is that the ending -*s* is added in the third person singular only, thus: *I go; you go; he/she/it goes; we go; you go; they go.* The verb *be* is an exception, with *am* in first person singular, *is* in third person singular and *are* everywhere else. Regional dialects have a variety of patterns which level out this paradigm: after all, the ending is redundant as a marker of person and number, given that this will be signalled by the subject pronoun or noun phrase. According to Trudgill (1999a: 101–2), East Anglian dialects tend to have no -*s* ending anywhere, thus *He like her; she want some; that rain a lot there*, but Northern and Western dialects have the -*s* ending throughout, as in *I wants it; he likes it; we sees them.* Where Northern dialects are concerned, the distribution of final -*s* is complicated by the 'Northern Subject Rule', according to which the verb takes -*s* in the plural where the subject is a noun or noun phrase, but not when it is a pronoun adjacent to the verb. Beal and Corrigan (2000) found this rule operating in Tyneside English. Examples from the NECTE corpus are: *Our young one's mates talks something like you* and *We visit her mam.* We found that the constraint against using the -*s* form after pronouns was particularly strong, but the use of -*s* after plural noun subjects was more common after conjoined nouns, as in: *Aye, and your sister and your mam comes out.*

3.3.3 Forms of be

The verb *be* is highly irregular in Standard English, with present tense forms *am/are/is* and past tense *was/were.* In both tenses, regional dialects display a range of different patterns. Taking data from the SED, Trudgill (1999a: 106–7) shows a geographical pattern for first person present tense forms whereby South-Western dialects have *be*;[5] Staffordshire and the 'Northern Southwest' have *bin*; the 'Lower North' has *is*; some parts of the South have *are*; and the rest of the country has *I am* as in Standard English. He goes on to explain this distribution as follows:

> The standard form *I am* thus occurs in a contiguous region comprising East Anglia, Lincolnshire, Leicestershire, South Yorkshire and Lancashire. There is a gap for the Lower North, which has *I is*, with *I am* resuming in the North (and on into Scotland). This division has

sometimes been explained as an intrusion into the Lower North of *is* as a Scandinavian form, and certainly the Lower North was an area of very high Viking Norwegian and Danish settlement. (1999a: 107)

As we shall see in Chapter 4, this distributional pattern is very common in lexical variation, where words of Norse origin tend to be most frequent in the 'Lower North'.

More research has been carried out into the patterns of variation in the past tense forms of *be*. As Britain (2002: 17) points out, 'virtually every vernacular variety of English appears to be variable with respect to past tense BE'. There are three main patterns: levelling to *was* (*I was; you was; he/she/it was; they was*); levelling to *were* (*I were; you were; he/she/it were; they were*); and levelling to *was* in positive contexts but *weren't* in negatives. The geographical distribution of these patterns is not straightforward, but some generalisations can be made. Cheshire et al. found that, whilst their survey respondents reported levelling to *was* throughout the country, it was 'less widespread ... in the urban centres of the North of England' and, conversely 'non-standard *were* was also reported frequently, in conjunction with non-standard *was*, by schools in the North-West, Yorkshire and Humberside, and in the East and West Midlands' (1993: 72). This distribution of non-standard *were* corresponds to that found by Ellis (1889), as reported in Britain (2002: 21): although there are isolated reports of it from various parts of the country, it seems to cluster around Cheshire, Derbyshire, Lancashire, Nottinghamshire and Yorkshire, in other words a continuous area of the 'Lower North', North-West and North-East Midlands. The continuing use of non-standard *were* in these areas is attested by Shorrocks (1999) and Moore (2003), both of whom conducted research in Bolton, and by Petyt (1985) and Richards (2008), both of whom found it in West Yorkshire, albeit largely in the language of working-class speakers. Moore's work is particularly important, as she finds the use of non-standard *were*, which might be considered a 'traditional' feature, used by adolescent girls as a marker of identity, a point to which we will return in Chapter 6. Cheshire et al. found non-standard *was* reported more frequently from the South of England, though there were some reports of non-standard *were* in this region too. They also found the *was/weren't* pattern in some urban centres, notably Birmingham. Since Tagliamonte (1998) and Britain (2002) report a shift towards this pattern in York and the Fens respectively, it may be the case that this is emerging as a 'levelled' or 'supra-localised' pattern.

3.3.4 Variation in the progressive

In Standard English, the use of progressive constructions, such as *I am reading a novel, I have been waiting for you*, etc., has expanded considerably over the last two hundred years (see Beal 2004: 78–82). Some regional dialects can perhaps be seen as conservative in using 'older' forms of the progressive, or avoiding it in some contexts, whilst others expand its use to contexts in which it is not found in Standard English. The form with *a-* as a prefix, identified by Kortmann (2008: 491) as confined to Southern dialects, was found in Standard English until the mid-eighteenth century, and so is a conservative feature. The avoidance of the progressive in sentences like *The kittle bile* ('The kettle's boiling') in traditional dialects of East Anglia (Trudgill 2008: 414) is likewise conservative.[6] On the other hand, the extension of the progressive in sentences such as *I'm liking this* and *What are you wanting* could be seen as innovative. Kortmann (2008: 491) identifies this as a Northern characteristic, but the first of these examples is becoming increasingly widespread, perhaps due to the influence of the current McDonald's slogan *I'm loving it.*

3.3.5 Contraction of negatives

In Section 3.2, we saw that what had been considered a general 'non-standard' feature, negative concord or multiple negation, is, in fact, more characteristic of speech in the South of England than that of the North. Another variable which has been identified as showing a North/South division is contraction of negatives. With auxiliary verbs such as *be, have, will* and *would*, negatives can undergo either negative contraction, e.g. *she isn't hasn't/won't/wouldn't*, or auxiliary contraction, e.g. *she's not* (for both *be* and *have)/she'll not/she'd not.* Hughes et al. suggest that auxiliary contraction is more common 'the further north one goes' (2005: 18). Both Anderwald (2002) and Tagliamonte and Smith (2002) find that this is not borne out in their comparative studies of negation in a range of regional dialects. Tagliamonte and Smith conclude that 'NEG/AUX contraction is a poor diagnostic for distinguishing varieties of British English on broad geographic grounds' (2002: 251).

Beal and Corrigan (2005b), however, comparing the findings of Anderwald and Tagliamonte and Smith with our own investigation of negation patterns in Tyneside English taken from the NECTE corpus, note that all three studies demonstrate similar patterns in Scotland and the North-East of England, with a higher rate of auxiliary contraction in these areas than elsewhere. With regard to auxiliary contraction of *will* in particular, the figures for Tagliamonte and Smith's data from County

Durham and Beal and Corrigan's from nearby Tyneside are almost identical at 70 per cent and 71.4 per cent respectively. I have pointed out elsewhere (1993: 187) that 'proximity to Scotland is reflected in the linguistic characteristics' of Tyneside and Northumbrian dialects. This linguistic continuity between dialects of the far North of England and those of Southern Scotland will be apparent at several points in this chapter and the next. All three of the studies mentioned here agree that, as far as negation of *be* is concerned, auxiliary contraction is much more common in all the regional varieties investigated, except in tag questions (*He's not coming* but *He's coming, isn't he?*). For *have*, both Tagliamonte and Smith and Beal and Corrigan find the reverse is the case, with negative contraction almost categorical even in the North-East. The preference for auxiliary contraction in this region seems to be confined to negation of *will*.

Some regional dialects display other patterns of contraction. In dialects of the Lower North, notably Lancashire and Yorkshire, there is also a pattern of secondary contraction, where both the auxiliary and the negator are contracted. Here, forms such as *isn't, couldn't, shouldn't* are contracted to /ɪnt, kʊnt, ʃʊnt/, etc., and *hasn't/hadn't* become homophonous as /ant/. These forms are attested by Petyt for West Yorkshire (1985: 179–89) and by Shorrocks for Bolton (1999: 153, 167, 172, 177). In the North-East, the negative of *do* can be *divvent*, which is found in Tyneside and Northumberland, or *dinnet* slightly further south in Sunderland (Burbano-Elizondo 2008), and, in traditional dialects of Northumberland, the negative of *will* can be *winnet*. In this area, uncontracted negatives are also found with some auxiliary verbs, especially *cannot*. Beal and Corrigan (2005b: 148) found that this was not the most common pattern, only occurring in just over 20 per cent of possible cases, and that speakers use the two forms interchangeably, as in *You can't change that. Cannot do anything about it*. Trudgill notes that 'interesting negative verb forms are widely found in the Staffordshire area. These are forms of *shan't, won't, can't* etc., which are formed from *no* rather than from *not*. Thus *shan't* is *shanno* or *shanna* and *didn't* is *didno* or *didna*' (1999a: 105). Although Trudgill only attributes these forms to Staffordshire, map 31 of the *Linguistic Atlas of England* (Orton et al. 1978) shows a wider distribution in the North-West Midlands, including Cheshire, Derbyshire and Shropshire.[7] That this is, at least locally, a well known feature of the 'Potteries' dialect is demonstrated by the presence of these and other auxiliaries with the *-na* ending in popular dialect literature, such as the 'Jabez' stories and the 'May and Mar Lady' cartoons which appear in the local newspaper the *Sentinel*. For instance, in the 'Jabez' story that appeared on 24 January 2001, we have:

Some o' th'posh folks *didna* larke th'road 'ey spok eether. Theyse folks reckoned yer *couldna* understand 'afe 'ey said if yer *wonna* born an' bred rind Aidley.[8] (my emphasis)

As we saw in Section 3.1, *ain't* as the negative form of both *have* and *be* is one of the features which Kortmann (2008: 491) lists as distinctively Southern. Thus, negated forms of auxiliary verbs are quite variable across regional dialects in England.

3.3.6 Patterns of negation in interrogatives and tags

In some Northern English dialects, negation in interrogatives and tags shows systematic variation between forms with contracted and uncontracted negators. Shorrocks (1999: 180–1) states that, in the Bolton dialect, a negative tag following a positive proposition is contracted, but following a negative proposition is uncontracted, as in: *It rained, didn't it?* versus *It didn't rain, did it not?* In the North-East, an even more complex pattern is found. A negative clause followed by **auxiliary + subject + not** is used when information is sought, as in: *She can't come, can she not?* But a negative clause followed by **auxiliary + n't + subject + not** is used when confirmation of the negative is sought, as in *She can't come, can't she not?* This pattern is also used in negative questions, where the speaker knows very well that the answer is *no*, but requires confirmation, possibly to settle a dispute with a third party. It is often used by children appealing to adult arbitration. An example would be *Can't Jack not ride a bike?* Here, what is implied is that everybody knows that Jack can't ride a bike, but Jack is denying this. A similar contrast occurs between two patterns for negative tags following positive clauses, with **auxiliary + subject + not** used when asking for information, and **auxiliary + n't + subject,** when asking for confirmation. Examples of these would be: *She can come, can she not?* and *She can come, can't she?*

All these examples are taken from McDonald and Beal (1987), but examples from the NECTE corpus are: *Had they not?; Oh, will you not be nice to her for once?; Did you not see the teeth?* In all of these, there is an element of surprise or exasperation: the uncontracted negative in an interrogative or tag has an emphatic force. In contrast to the elaborate patterns found in these Northern dialects, some Southern dialects have an invariant tag *innit/in't it/isn't it* whatever the auxiliary in the preceding clause. Although Kortmann (2008: 491) lists this as one of his predominantly Southern features, it is mainly found as an emerging feature in adolescent London speech, possibly introduced from Indian and/or Jamaican English in this multicultural city.

3.3.7 Periphrastic do

We saw in Section 3.1 that both Wakelin (1983) and Ihalainen (1994) cite periphrastic *do* as a distinguishing feature of South-Western dialects. In Standard English, *do* as an auxiliary verb only appears in positive declarative sentences when it is emphatic, as in *I **did** tell you!*, or to avoid repetition of another verb, as in *He told you and so did I.* The use of unstressed *do* in sentences such as *She did do a lot of needlework* and *William, my son, do live down there* (Wagner 2008: 435) was found in Standard English until about 1700, but is now, within England, confined to the South-West. It is also found in Welsh and Irish varieties of English, leading some to suggest that this feature may have an origin in a Celtic substratum or in Celtic–English language contact.[9] Where periphrastic *do* is used, it either expresses habitual aspect, or acts as an analytic tense-carrier. Wagner analysed the use of periphrastic *do* in the South-Western texts from the FRED corpus and concluded that it 'is omnipresent with some speakers, whilst others do not have it in their language system at all' (2008: 435).

3.3.8 Modal verbs

Kortmann's (2008: 491) list of features which distinguish dialects of the North of Britain from those of the South includes two that involve modal verbs: double modals and epistemic *mustn't*. There is a 'rule' of Standard English that only one modal verb can appear in a single verb phrase. Thus, *He must be able to do it* is 'grammatical' whilst *He must can do it* is not. In North-Eastern dialects of English, this rule does not apply so long as the second modal is *can* or *could*. Thus the asterisked sentence would be grammatical in these dialects. There seems to be a North–South cline of acceptability for double modals: more combinations of modals are allowed in Scots than in North-Eastern English dialects, and more are allowed in the dialect of rural Northumberland than in that of urban Tyneside. For instance, the combination of *would* and *could* only appears in the urban area if a negative is involved, but also appears in the positive in rural Northumberland. Examples from McDonald (1981: 186–7) are:

I can't play on a Friday. I work late. I might could get it changed, though.

The girls usually make me some (toasted sandwiches) but they mustn't could have made any today.

He wouldn't could've worked, even if you had asked him. (Tyneside)

A good machine clipper would could do it in half a day. (Northumberland)

Double modals appear to be recessive in the north of England. McDonald (1981) found that 15.42 per cent of respondents from north of Durham found sentences with double modals were either wholly acceptable or normal or somewhere between these two. In a later survey, Beal and Corrigan (2000) found that only 9.37 per cent of a sample of 16–17-year-olds from Bedlington, Northumberland, found the same sentences either 'natural' or 'familiar', whilst 90.63 per cent found them 'alien'. The acceptability of the constructions was higher amongst working-class children, who may well still hear them used by their grandparents.

Unlike double modals, epistemic *mustn't* shows no sign of receding in the North of England. In the North-East, *mustn't* rather than *can't* would normally be used to express the notion 'the evidence leads me to conclude ... that' as in *The lift mustn't be working* (McDonald and Beal 1987). Shorrocks (1999: 157) notes that this use of *mustn't* is 'permitted' in the dialect of Bolton. In the North-East, obligation is expressed by *have got to* in both positive and negative sentences. Thus, *you haven't got to* means 'you are obliged not to', whereas in Standard English and other dialects it would mean 'you are not obliged to'. Finally, whilst *shall* is rarely used in any dialect of English, or even in colloquial Standard English, in most dialects it is used in first person questions, such as *Shall I make you a cup of tea?* In the North-East, as in Scotland and Ireland, *will* is used even in this context: *Will I make you a cup of tea?* In many ways, then, the modal system of dialects in the far North of England is more similar to those of Irish and Scots English than to more southerly dialects in England. The 'Middle North' shares some of these characteristics, such as a tolerance for epistemic *mustn't*.

3.3.9 Complementation

In earlier (Standard) English, the infinitive could be introduced by *for to* rather than simply *to*, and this persists in both the South-West and the North. According to Wagner (2008: 432), in the South-West *for to* is used to introduce purpose clauses, but in the North it can introduce any infinitive clauses, as in *When I moved it just didn't enter me head for to say I wonder what if it'll be different* (from the NECTE corpus) and, from Bolton, *We were glad for to get out* (Shorrocks 1999: 248).

There are different patterns of complementation after the verbs *need* and *want* in regional dialects of English. In the North-East, these are followed by a past participle, as *My hair needs washed; The cat wants fed*, whereas elsewhere the present participle or passive infinitive would be used, thus *My hair needs washing/ to be washed; The cat wants feeding/ to be fed*.

3.4 Regional variation in the noun phrase

3.4.1 Noun morphology

There are few regionally distinct patterns of noun morphology. In most dialects, there is a tendency for nouns referring to quantities or measurements, such as *pound*, *mile*, etc., to lack an overt plural marker, especially after numerals, where it would be redundant. Cheshire et al. included examples of unmarked plurals in their survey and concluded that 'absence of plural marking is indeed very widespread in urban varieties of English' (1993: 67) but that some nouns are more likely to be unmarked than others. For nouns other than those of measurement, Wagner notes that 'West Country dialects at one time preferred the traditional *-en* ending over the StE *-s*, but have since adopted the StE strategy', but that, for some nouns ending in /sC/, these dialects use '[ɪz] as a form of consonant cluster simplification', as in *ghostes* or *beasties* (2008: 419). In the North, plural nouns sometimes take an extra 's in the possessive, as in *it's other folks's* (Shorrocks 1999: 64).

3.4.2 Second person pronouns

There is a good deal of variation between the pronoun systems of regional dialects in England. We have already seen in Section 3.1 that Ihalainen (1994: 231) identifies 'pronoun exchange' as characteristic of South-Western dialects, whilst Kortmann (2008: 491) includes 'special forms or phrases for the second person plural pronoun' in his list of characteristically 'Northern' features. As we shall see, neither of these features has such a straightforward geographical distribution. The personal pronoun paradigm of Standard English is set out in Table 3.1.

Table 3.1 Personal pronouns in Standard English.

Person/Gender	Number	Subject	Object	Possessive
1st	Singular	I	me	my
1st	Plural	we	us	our
2nd	Singular	you	you	your
2nd	Plural	you	you	your
3rd masculine	Singular	he	him	his
3rd feminine	Singular	she	her	her
3rd neuter	Singular	it	it	its
3rd M/F/N	Plural	they	them	their

What is apparent here is that not all distinctions are overtly marked. The second person paradigm is particularly noticeable in this respect:

singular and plural, subject and object are all identical. This is due to a historical process whereby these distinctions have been neutralised in present-day Standard English. In Middle English these distinctions were all marked, as in Table 3.2.

Table 3.2 Second person pronouns in Middle English.

Number	Subject	Object
Singular	thou	thee
Plural	ye	you

What complicated matters was the introduction, from the thirteenth century, and almost certainly under the influence of French, of the tendency to use *ye/you* as 'polite' forms of address to a single person. This never functioned in exactly the same way as French *vous*, and there is a considerable amount of scholarship devoted to the study of the social nuances reflected in variation between *thou/thee* and *ye/you* forms in sixteenth- and seventeenth-century literature. The distinction between *ye* as subject and *you* as object form was likewise neutralised in this period, so that, by about 1700, the second person pronoun paradigm in Standard English was more or less as it is today.[10]

The subject/object distinction is no great loss pragmatically, since it is marked syntactically: *you like her* vs. *she likes you*. The loss of singular/plural distinction is more problematic: unless there is only one other person present, speakers of Standard English have to rely on eye-contact, gestures, personal names or phrases such as *you two/lot/guys/on the back row*, etc., to signal exactly to whom they are speaking. As Katie Wales points out, 'many dialect speakers … have felt the loss of a singular–plural distinction in standard English to be a disadvantage, and so have initiated new plurals' (2006: 19), whilst others retain the old singular forms *thou* and *thee*. Although both Kortmann (2008) and Wales (2006) identify the plural form *yous(e)* as Northern, it would perhaps be more accurate to describe its distribution as urban. Cheshire et al. note that 'schools in the core of the Manchester metropolitan region consistently reported the occurrence of the pronoun *youse*, whereas schools elsewhere in the region did not' (1993: 81). The use of *youse* as a second person plural pronoun was almost certainly introduced from Irish English. Wright (1898–1905) cites it as occurring in Ireland, the USA and Australia, but not yet in England or Scotland. We need to bear in mind here that Wright's *English Dialect Dictionary* dealt mainly with 'traditional' rural dialects, and so would not have recorded the presence of *yous(e)* in urban varieties, but the first instances recorded in the *Oxford English*

Dictionary (*OED*) are from Irish English, and the regional English varieties in which it first appears are all in cities with a high level of Irish immigration from the nineteenth century onwards: Liverpool, Newcastle and inner-city Manchester. The NECTE corpus contains several instances of *yous*, mainly from younger speakers recorded in 1994. Examples are:

> *Yous'll have Thomas next year.* ('Thomas' being the surname of a teacher and *yous* referring to the whole class)

> *Yous* can come up any time … because like it's ours now … but *yous* like, *yous* all have to contribute to the gas and stuff but … not too bad

All three of the northern cities in which *yous* has been attested are close to areas in which, at least amongst older and/or rural speakers, *thou/thee* forms of the second person singular are used. Evidence from the SED, collected from older, rural speakers in the 1950s, shows *thou* to have been widespread everywhere north of the Humber (except in Northumberland and northern County Durham, where *ye* occurs); in Cheshire, Derbyshire and parts of Nottinghamshire and Lincolnshire; and in most of the South-West and West Midlands, except along the Welsh border (Upton and Widdowson 1996: 66–7). Wales (2003–4: 177) states that 'in the "Black Country" round Wolverhampton and Dudley near Birmingham *thee*- subjective and objective forms are still heard amongst the elderly'. There is also evidence that *thee/thou* forms are still used in parts of the North, albeit often in formulaic phrases such as the stereotypical Yorkshire leave-taking *Sithee* ('I'll see you'). The following examples are from Sheffield and Bolton respectively:

> But before I went into this job I was just like him off that thing that we were on about South-Yorkshire, all thees and thas …

> It's no use thee going down, is it? (Shorrocks 1999: 79)

The Sheffield example, recorded in 1981, shows that the use of *thee/thou* was already a stereotype: the speaker is not using these pronouns, but citing them as typical of 'South Yorkshire'. Indeed, in the Sheffield area a verbal form *thee-ing and tha-ing* (cf. French *tutoyer*) is used to describe this usage, in the saying:

> Thee thee and tha me and I'll thee and tha thee and thee thee and tha thyself and see how tha likes it.

This implies that, just as in most European languages and in earlier English, use of *thee/thou* is socially marked and inappropriate use can offend. Cave (2001), in an ethnographic study of the language of the former mining community in Barnsley, South Yorkshire, found that use of *thou/thee* forms was confined to men in the corpus he collected, but that the wives of the former miners admitted to using these forms to their husbands in a domestic setting. Shorrocks also found *thou/thee* forms used for the second person singular in Bolton, and some evidence that *you* is still used as a polite form in the singular: 'there are still sons in the Bolton area who appear to use only the *yo* form when addressing their fathers' (1999: 74).

In the North, then, the pattern of second person pronoun usage is that *thou/thee* as a singular and/or 'intimate' form persists in some areas, whilst *yous* is found in some of the larger conurbations, especially those with a history of Irish immigration. In the North-East, *ye* persists as the subject form of the second person singular, and there are even some speakers who make the four-way distinction *ye/you/yees/yous* (Beal 1993: 205). Elsewhere, the second person plural form *you … together* is found in East Anglia, and *thee* still occurs in the West Midlands and South-West, though it appears to be recessive here.

3.4.3 Pronoun exchange

'Pronoun exchange' is the term used to refer to a phenomenon whereby what would, in Standard English, be the subject form is used in object position and vice versa. On the basis of the SED material, Ihalainen suggests that this 'is one of the few features that divide the country up in an east–west direction' (1994: 231). However, Trudgill (1999a: 95) and Beal (1993, 2004) find elements of pronoun exchange in Essex and the North-East respectively. This distribution suggests, as Trudgill points out, that pronoun exchange was formerly more widespread and has now receded to these areas. In the North-East, only first person plural forms are 'exchanged', and it is much more common for *we* (pronounced /wə/) to be used in object position than *us* in subject position, but both are attested, as the examples below demonstrate:

You can come with we to that as well.

Us'll do it

Pronoun exchange is much more extensive in the South-West, in that it occurs in both first and third persons, as can be seen in the examples below from the FRED corpus (Wagner 2008: 421):

I did give she a 'and and she did give I a 'and and we did 'elp one another

Well, if I didn't know they, they knowed I

Never had no fault at all with she

Evercreech, what did 'em call it?

We used to stook it off, didn't us?

The consensus amongst scholars who have studied pronoun exchange is that subject forms are used for emphasis, and object forms elsewhere. Wagner finds examples such as those cited above, but concludes that, even in the South-West, pronoun exchange is recessive. In the North-East, what looks like a relic of pronoun exchange may well have become simply a local form of the first person plural.

3.4.4 'Gendered' pronouns

Standard English and, indeed, most regional dialects in England have a system of natural gender, whereby, with the exception of personifications and affective usage, masculine pronouns are used to refer to animate males, feminine ones to animate females, and neuter ones for inanimate objects and some animals. Old English, like many modern languages, had a system of grammatical gender, so that inanimate objects could take masculine or feminine pronouns, according to the class of noun. In the South-West, there is what appears to be a relic of grammatical gender: whilst non-count nouns always take *it*, inanimate count nouns take *he*. Examples (from Wagner 2008: 425) are:

I bet thee cansn climb he [= tree]

He do go now. He 'ave been a good watch.

Wagner finds that 'gendered' pronouns are less recessive in the South-West than pronoun exchange, and that they are most widespread in Devon and Cornwall. She also makes the interesting observation that 'while most non-standard varieties of English world-wide have extended feminine forms to inanimate ... referents ..., this task is still fulfilled by masculine forms in West Country speech, making it almost unique amongst English dialects' (2008: 427).

3.4.5 Relative markers

In Standard English, there are three different ways of marking the relative. The use of these is constrained by whether the antecedent is animate or inanimate; whether the clause is restrictive (specifying the antecedent) or non-restrictive (simply adding information about the antecedent); and whether the antecedent is subject, object or possessor. In all types of sentence, relative pronouns, or *wh*-relatives, may be used. These are *who, whom, whose, which* according to case and animacy. Examples are:

- The professor who taught linguistics has retired. (restrictive, animate, subject)
- Professor Morrissey, who taught linguistics, has retired. (non-restrictive, animate, subject)
- The professor who(m) I met last night taught linguistics. (restrictive, animate, object)
- Professor Morrissey, who(m) I met last night, taught linguistics. (non-restrictive, animate, object)
- The class which Professor Morrissey taught was really interesting. (restrictive, inanimate, object)
- Linguistics 101, which Professor Morrissey taught, was really interesting. (non-restrictive, inanimate, object)
- The class which was most interesting was Linguistics 101. (restrictive, inanimate, subject)
- Linguistics 101, which was the most interesting class, got the best feedback. (non-restrictive, inanimate, subject)
- The professor whose best class was Linguistics 101 has retired. (animate, possessive, restrictive)
- Professor Morrissey, whose best class was Linguistics 101, has retired. (animate, possessive, non-restrictive)
- The class whose students always got the best results was Linguistics 101. (inanimate, possessive, restrictive)
- Linguistics 101, whose students always got the best results, was taught by Professor Morrissey. (inanimate, possessive, non-restrictive)

In restrictive relatives, *that* can be used mainly though not exclusively with inanimate or non-human antecedents. Examples follow (those marked with a question mark would be unacceptable to some speakers of Standard English):

- The professor that taught linguistics has retired? (animate, subject, restrictive)
- The professor that I met last night taught linguistics? (animate, object, restrictive)
- The class that Professor Morrissey taught was really interesting. (inanimate, object, restrictive)
- The class that was most interesting was Linguistics 101. (inanimate, subject, restrictive)

In less formal Standard English, the zero relative (marked here with Ø) can be used with object antecedents in restrictive clauses only, thus:

- The professor Ø I met last night taught linguistics. (animate, object, restrictive)
- The class Ø Professor Morrissey taught was really interesting. (inanimate, object, restrictive)

There is a cline of formality in these examples from the most formal *wh-* relatives to the least formal zero. Romaine (1982), who conducted the first sociohistorical study of relative markers in English, finds that the *wh-* relative markers (*who, whom, whose, which*) occur first (from the fifteenth century onwards) in more formal, particularly Latinate, styles and the nominative type (*who, which*) is confined to formal usage for longer than the object or genitive types. She goes on to assert that 'infiltration of WH into the relative system … has not really affected the spoken language' (1982: 212).

Since the introduction of the *wh-* relatives was a change 'from above', we might expect them to be rarer in regional dialects. This was certainly the case in the SED materials: the SED questionnaire elicited forms of the relative with subject antecedent by asking informants to complete the following:

The woman next door says: The work in this garden is getting me down. You say: Well, get some help in. I know a man … will do it for you. (IX.9.5)

The man … looks after the cows (III.3.7)

For the first of these, the forms elicited were zero, *as*, *at*, *that* and *what*. Zero was the most widespread, which is not surprising as sentences beginning with *I know, there's*, etc. could have zero relative in informal Standard English today. *As* was recorded only in Cumberland, Lancashire and Yorkshire; *at* mainly in the North, but also in Essex; *that* again in the North, but also in Staffordshire and Middlesex; and there was only one instance of *what*, in Lancashire. In answers to the second question, zero was less widespread, occurring in the South and East Anglia; *as* occurred almost everywhere except the far North, where *at* was used; and *what* was fairly widespread, but was not found in the North except for parts of Yorkshire that would now be in Humberside.

The use of *what* appears to have spread northwards since the time of the SED: although Kortmann (2008: 491) includes *what* in his list of definitively Southern features, he notes that it is now also found in the

North of England (though not Scotland or Ireland). Cheshire et al. report that, in the results from the Survey of British Dialect Grammar 'relative *what* was reported just as frequently in Glasgow and the North of England as in the South ... *What*, then, appears to be the preferred relative pronoun in the urban centres of Britain today' (1993: 68). However, Beal and Corrigan (2005a), comparing results from corpora of Tyneside and Sheffield English collected in the second half of the twentieth century, find *what* to be much rarer in the Tyneside material, but well attested in Sheffield. Examples from the Corpus of Sheffield Usage (CSU) are:

> We listen to Radio Sheffield to all t'news **what**'s going off you know (CSU 008)

> It's double t'money **what** you're getting at home (CSU 014)

The discrepancy between these results from corpus data and those from the Survey of British Dialect Grammar could reflect the fact that the latter elicited judgements from children, who could be reporting forms that they had heard (e.g. on television) rather than those that they would actually use. The frequency of *what* in the Sheffield corpus data does suggest that this has spread either northwards, or westwards from Humberside, since the time of the SED.

The other regional relative markers today are *as* and *at*: Wagner (2008: 429) notes that *as* is found in the South-West, though not as frequently as *what*, and Shorrocks states that it is 'the chief relative pronoun in the dialect [of Bolton]' (1999: 98). Examples from these two areas are:

> My dear sister as is dead and gone (Wagner 2008: 429)

> Thou knows Jimmy, him as were deaf? (Shorrocks 1999: 98)

At was formerly widespread in Yorkshire, but seems to be recessive now: there were few instances of it in the CSU, and Petyt (1985: 201) notes that in his corpus of West Yorkshire speech '[ðat] occurred 1250 times altogether in conversational styles, while the non-standard [at] and [az] were heard 234 and 21 times respectively'. It would appear that *what* and *that* are becoming more widespread as relative markers for all cases and for animate and inanimate antecedents, but *what* is less frequent in the far North.

The use and distribution of relative markers in regional dialects differ from those in Standard English in other respects, but these tend not to be regionally differentiated. The tendency to use zero with subject antecedents, especially when introduced by *I know* as in the SED example, or *I've, there's* as in the examples below from Sheffield, Tyneside and the South-West respectively, is a feature of all regional dialects in England, and even of informal Standard English.

I've a mother ø's still living, she's a widow (CSU 017)

I've a sister ø's over there, she loves stotties (TLS G52)

There's a pair of blocks down there was made when I was apprentice (Wagner 2008: 430)

3.4.6 Demonstrative pronouns

In Standard English, demonstrative pronouns distinguish between referents that are close (literally or metaphorically) and those that are distant, and between singular and plural, as in Table 3.3.

Table 3.3 Demonstratives in Standard English.

Close, singular	Close, plural	Distant, singular	Distant, plural
this	these	that	those

Regional dialects differ with regard to both the forms of demonstratives and the systems of contrasts expressed by them. Some dialects differentiate three degrees of distance: whereas Standard English has 'close' and 'distant', these have a third term meaning 'more distant'. In Standard English, this concept has to be expressed by circumlocutions such as 'that one over there'. In the SED materials, expressions for 'that over there' are found in the North, where *yon* and *thon* were used, and in the South-West, where forms like *thick* and *thicker* occurred. However, these South-Western forms were always found with 'over there', suggesting that they no longer operated to express far distance, as they needed to be reinforced by the same kind of circumlocution found in Standard English. Wagner agrees that 'examples of a threefold distinction are either non-existent or difficult to find' (2008: 427). In the North, the use of *yon* as a measure of far distance was quite extensive in the SED materials, but Shorrocks (1999: 54) notes that *yon* refers not to something distant, but to a 'known referent': *yon mon* may refer to a man not present, but known to all interlocutors, or easily identified from the preceding conversation. It would appear that systems with three terms are relics and are no longer really functional even in those dialects, i.e. those of the North and South-West, which retain the distinctive terms. South-Western dialects do, however, distinguish between forms relating to count and non-count nouns, with *thick, thicky* used for the former and *this, that* for the latter. Standard English *those* tends not to be used in regional dialects, where *them* is widespread, and *they* is found in the far North.

3.4.7 The definite article

Northern dialects are distinctive with regard to the forms of the definite article and the circumstances in which it occurs. One feature which is often regarded as stereotypically northern is definite article reduction, whereby *the* is pronounced as /t/, /θ/ or a glottal stop, or is not pronounced at all. This is not found in the far North-East: in the SED materials it is absent from Northumberland, except in *tother*, which is probably lexicalised, as *the tother* was found in Northumberland and elsewhere, 'thus making what is, historically, a double definite article' (Upton et al. 1994: 481). Today, definite article reduction is not found in the North-East north of the Tees: it is generally recognised as a stereotype of Yorkshire and Lancashire speech, but also occurs in Northern parts of the Midlands, especially Cheshire, Derbyshire and Nottinghamshire. The reduction to /θ/ appears to be more common in Lancashire than in Yorkshire: Petyt (1985) and Shorrocks (1999) both collected their data in the 1970s, from West Yorkshire and Bolton, Lancashire, respectively. Whilst Petyt found the glottal stop to be the commonest variant, Shorrocks notes 'there are no exceptions to the use of /θ/ before a vowel/diphthong' (1999: 29). The catchphrase of Bolton comedian Peter Kay, 'In th'ouse on t'internet', bears witness to the fact that this is still common. Zero forms are more widespread in East Yorkshire: the 'zero definite article' is one of a number of dialect features 'widely represented' in Tagliamonte's corpus of York English (Tagliamonte and Ito 2002: 245–6), and Jones (2002: 342) suggests that this represents the final stage in a historical process of reduction from /θ/ → /t/ → /ʔ/ → zero.

In the North-East, the full form of the definite article is used in contexts where it would not appear in Standard English. Although the SED materials show that the use of *the* with the names of ailments or diseases, such as *the headache*, was fairly widespread, in dialects of the North-East of England, the definite article is used with a much wider range of nouns. These include names of institutions, illnesses, periods of time, games, relatives and even numerals. Examples from the NECTE corpus are:

Going over to the girlfriend's concert first though.

So what are you doing in college the morrow?

I think Karen and Kell are going down there the-night.

So I never really started work 'til I was about the fifteen.

Well, I've got a little laddie that gans to the Beacon Lough. ('Beacon Lough' is the name of a school)

Although other studies of northern dialects show no evidence of this, Shorrocks (1999: 31–42) gives examples (with definite article reduction) in all the categories mentioned above. It is possible that these uses of the definite article were formerly more widespread throughout the North, or, indeed, that they exist elsewhere in the North but have not been captured by other dialect surveys. These uses of the definite article are also found in Scots and Irish English: Kortmann notes that 'unusual uses of the definite article are reported for Orkney and Shetland, the North and in Celtic Englishes' (2008: 488).

3.5 Summary

Although this has been a fairly comprehensive study of morphological and syntactic differences between regional dialects in England, there are features that have not been discussed, either because they are confined to a small area, or because they are so common as to be 'non-standard' rather than regional. In the former category, I would include features such as the use of *while* for Standard English *(un)til* in Yorkshire ('We're open nine while five'), and widespread non-standard features would include, for instance, double marking of comparatives and superlatives, as in:

Because you were more fitter.

She's got the most loveliest clothes.

It must be said, however, that there is much work still to be done investigating the syntax and morphology of regional dialects: as we saw in Section 3.2, multiple negation had been assumed to be a universal non-standard feature until Anderwald (2002, 2005) discovered that it is less common in the North. There are also parts of the country in which little research has been carried out since the SED: for instance, Kortmann and Upton (2008) contains no chapter on the morphology and syntax of dialects in the Midlands.

What is noticeable is that the most distinctive dialects, as far as morphology and syntax are concerned, are those of the North, especially the North-East, and the South-West. These are the areas most distant from London, and so, until very recently, would be the last to be affected by the diffusion of innovations from the capital and the surrounding area. There are similarities between the dialects of the North-East and Scotland, due to geographical contiguity and close historical relationships (see Beal 1993: 187–8), and differences between dialects of the 'far North' (north of the Tees) and those of Lancashire, Yorkshire and the North Midlands which may be due to the greater influence of contact with Scandinavian languages in what was formerly the Danelaw (see Figure 4.2). The South-West, on the other hand, retains archaic features such as grammatical gender, perhaps because this area, like the far North, was outside the Danelaw. Innovative features, such as plural *yous*, can appear to be 'scattered' geographically, but may be attributable to more recent language contact in larger towns and cities. All these language-external factors will need to be borne in mind in the next chapter, when we look at lexical differences between English regional dialects.

Exercises

The table on page 51 provides twenty-three sentences, each of which contains a feature of non-standard grammar.

- Consider whether you use forms like this often, use them occasionally, don't use them but have heard them, or have never used or heard them, and tick the boxes accordingly.
- Compare your answers with those of others in your class.
- Are any of the features specific to particular regional dialects, and, if so, do the people who have said they use the features come from those regions?
- Do you think that some of the features are more widespread and/or likely to be found in less formal usage?
- Do you think any of these features are more likely to be used by younger or older speakers?
- If you do use any of these features, in what contexts would you use them (formal/informal; spoken/written; with which groups of people)?

Further reading

Trudgill and Chambers (1991) and Milroy and Milroy (1993) provide studies of morphosyntactic variation in a range of varieties of English. A more recent and comprehensive survey is provided in Kortmann and Upton (2008). Kortmann et al. (2005) is a collection of corpus-based studies of grammatical variation in the British Isles focusing on agreement, relativisation and gender. Anderwald (2002) provides a corpus-

	I often use forms like this	I occasionally use forms like this	I never use forms like this but I've heard them used	I never use forms alike this and I've never heard them used
1 *We **don't** do **nothing** exciting round here*				
2 *That **int** working*				
3 *He **ain't** got any*				
4 *He broke that – I **never**.*				
5 *Is that the one I **seen** last night?*				
6 *I've **give** him the water already*				
7 *I **drawed** a cool picture*				
8 *He **done** it wrong*				
9 *I **likes** dancing*				
10 *She **like** the picture*				
11 *I **weren't** happy about going out*				
12 *Me and Sam **was** having a party*				
13 *He **might could** do it*				
14 *The cat **needs fed***				
15 *I've come **for't fix** the boiler*				
16 *That was the thing **what** did my head in*				
17 *Did he hurt **hisself**?*				
18 *He's crazy, **him***				
19 *He's stupid, **is Sam***				
20 *Look at **them** big dogs*				
21 *He's **well nicer** than you*				
22 *I like pasta – it cooks really **quick***				
23 *That bloke is **five foot** tall*				

based study of negation in varieties of British English, and Iyeiri (2005) is a collection of papers including some dealing with negation in English dialects. Anderwald (2009) is a study of irregular verb forms in English dialects.

Notes

1. In fact, there are many more studies of morphological and syntactic variation within and between dialects of English. The references here simply indicate some of the key scholars working on varieties within England. Most of these have also studied varieties in other parts of the UK and the English-speaking world.
2. The 'observer's paradox' was formulated by William Labov as follows: 'the aim of linguistic research in the community must be to find out how people talk when they are not being systematically observed; yet we can only obtain these data by systematic observation' (1972: 209).
3. In fact, the North-East was the exception to the rule in Anderwald's study, with a higher percentage of tokens of negative concord than other regions in the North and Midlands. Beal and Corrigan, however, find a percentage (6 per cent) much closer to that found by Anderwald in other Northern regions.
4. For a full description and classification of these verbal paradigms in Standard English, see Quirk et al. (1985: 104).
5. 'Finite *be*' is, of course, one of the features used by Wakelin (1983) and Ihalainen (1994) to distinguish dialects of the South-West from those of the rest of England.
6. Compare this with Shakespeare's use of 'What do you read, my Lord?' (*Hamlet* II.ii.190). Here, Polonius comes upon Hamlet, who is reading. In present-day Standard English, Polonius would say 'What are you reading, my Lord?'
7. Thanks to Derek Britton for pointing this out.
8. 'Some of the posh folks didn't like the way he spoke either. These folks reckoned you couldn't understand half they said if you weren't born and bred round Aidley.' Thanks to Chris Montgomery for this example, and for confirming that as a native of Stoke he is familiar with *conna* and *wonna*.
9. See Filppula et al. (2008: 230–2) for a discussion of this.
10. See Nevalainen (2006: 78–80) for a summary of this.

4 Dialect variation in England: lexis

4.1 Introduction

Although the efforts of nineteenth-century dialectologists were concentrated on the production of dialect dictionaries, and, as we saw in
Chapter 1, the recent BBC Voices project elicited a massive response to
its appeal for regional vocabulary, the study of regional lexis has been the
'Cinderella' of academic dialectology in the late twentieth and early
twenty-first centuries. Ihalainen (1994: 248) cites Glauser (1974), Fischer
(1976) and Viereck (1986) as the exceptions which demonstrate that
'in spite of occasional reservations by dialectologists, lexical material
can be used to define dialect areas'. All three of these studies are based
on evidence from the SED, but the first two are confined to specific
areas: the English–Scottish border and the South-West of England
respectively. Only Viereck attempts to use lexical evidence to produce
nationwide dialect divisions.

The comprehensive volume on varieties of English in the British Isles
edited by Kortmann and Upton (2008) is divided into two sections: the
first devoted to phonology and the second to morphology and syntax.
Where lexis is discussed at all, it is either with reference to grammati-
calised items such as focusing and quotative *like*, or as a short final section
in some chapters in the second section (see, for instance, Beal (2008:
399–401; Sebba 2008: 475–6). Hughes et al. (2005) likewise pay little
attention to lexis. In an eighteen-page chapter on dialect variation, the
section on lexical features consists of just seven lines, and in the sections
devoted to individual regional varieties, comments on lexis are included
in notes on the recordings, and take the form of glosses. One of the more
extensive notes on lexis can be found in the section on Liverpool, reproduced below.

There are some perhaps unfamiliar lexical items:

bob (l. 22) = a shilling (twelve pence) in pre-decimal currency. The
term continued to be used after decimalization in 1971, and in fact the

shilling piece was used for some years after this as the equivalent of five new pence.

made up (l. 41) = very pleased.

tap (l. 23) = take money from.

well away (l. 31) = drunk.

where it is (l. 19) = *the thing is.* (Hughes et al. 2005: 101)

One reason for this relative neglect of lexical variation is that dialect studies moved away from the historical approach of the SED and the early dialect dictionaries to focus on typology. We saw in Chapter 2 that the dialects of England have tended to be classified on the basis of phonological and, to a lesser extent, morphological and syntactic factors. Whilst the more extensive set of criteria provided in Kortmann and Upton (2008) provide a more equal balance between phonology and morphology/syntax, they still include no lexical criteria for the comparison of dialects. This is probably because it is much more difficult to make generalisations about the regional distribution of lexis. The fact that *bairn* is used in the North of England has no implications for the distribution of other words: in the phrase attributed to Jules Gilliéron, author of the *Atlas linguistique de la France, chaque mot a son histoire* ('every word has its own history'). However, as we shall see in the following section, it is possible to see regional trends in the use of words from particular sources where these reflect historical patterns of contact.

4.2 Patterns of lexical variation

The SED elicited a great deal of lexical information, and several publications present and discuss this. Orton and Wright (1974), Upton et al. (1987) and Upton and Widdowson (1996) all include maps based on the SED data, and Upton et al. (1994) presents the data in the form of a dictionary. These sources allow us to look for patterns in the distribution of dialect words. These may reflect historical patterns of language contact, where influence from other languages is evident, or the relative conservatism of certain regions, where words that were formerly more widespread are now restricted to isolated areas.

4.2.1 Words of Scandinavian origin

Perhaps the most easily identified pattern of historical contact is that described as the 'Great Scandinavian Belt', defined by Samuels (1985: 269) as 'a belt stretching from Cumberland and Westmoreland in the west to the North and East Ridings of Yorkshire in the east, often including parts of Lincolnshire but excluding the old kingdom of

Bernicia in Durham and Northumberland'. Dialects of the 'Scandinavian Belt' are characterised by the density of words of Norse origin, just as the topography of this area is notable for the density of Norse place-names. This area is within what was known as the Danelaw, the part of England ceded to Danish control under the Treaty of Alfred and Guthrum in 884, so it is easy to see how contact between speakers of Scandinavian and Northern English dialects has affected the modern dialect vocabulary.

Orton and Wright (1974: 17) note that 'several thousands of Scandinavian loans are found in the present-day dialects of the North and East Midlands', examples being *addled* for 'earned', *femmer* for 'brittle', *garth* for 'yard', *ket* for 'rubbish', *lake* for 'play', *lops* for 'fleas' and *slape* for 'slippery'. These words vary in their distribution: *lops* is found in the east of the region, and further north than other Scandinavian words, extending into Northumberland, whilst *lake, addled* and *slape* are more closely confined within the 'Scandinavian Belt'. One word which illustrates the typical distribution of Scandinavian loan-words in Northern English dialects is *beck*. The question put to SED informants in order to elicit this term and its synonyms in other dialects was 'What do you call any running water smaller than a river?', and the results can be seen on Figure 4.1. If we compare this with Figure 4.2, illustrating the division of England between King Alfred and the Danes, we can see that the area in which *beck* is used is that in which Scandinavian influence was most extensive. North of this area, in Northumberland (and, of course, in Scotland), the Old English word *burn* is used, whilst to the south and west, another Old English word, *brook*, occurs. Unlike some of the other Scandinavian-derived words cited above, *beck* is still known and used, as are *burn* and *brook* in their respective areas, although all three compete with Standard English *stream*. The dialect words are also found in place-names in the relevant areas, such as Otterburn in Northumberland, Troutbeck in Cumbria and Cressbrook in Derbyshire.

4.2.2 Words of French origin

In contrast to the Scandinavian invasions and settlements, the Norman Conquest of 1066 has left its mark more on the vocabulary of Standard English than on regional dialects. Orton and Wright (1974: 22) note that, again in contrast to the clear regional distribution of Scandinavian words, where French words are concerned 'the patterns of distribution … are inconsistent', some suggesting that 'French words are more extensively used in the South than the North', but others being found in the North only.

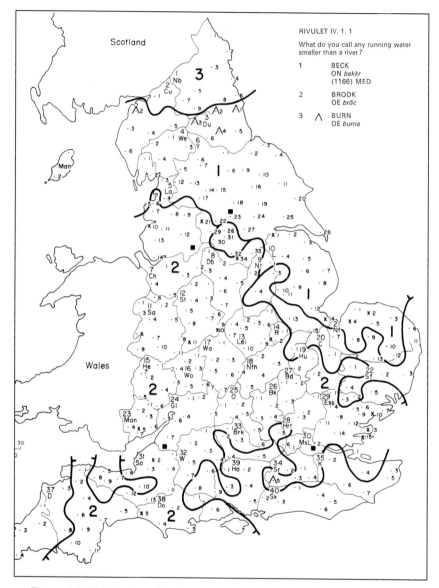

Figure 4.1 Distribution of *beck*, *brook* and *burn* in SED (from Orton and Wright 1974: 87).

Figure 4.2. The Danelaw (from Barber et al. 2009: 139).

In fact, many of the French/Anglo-Norman words which show a Southern distribution in Orton and Wright's maps have become Standard English, examples being *collar* (for a horse), *beak* and *braces*, for which Northern dialects have *bargham*, *neb* and *gallows* respectively. The most likely explanation here is that Southern dialects did indeed adopt more words from (Norman) French in the Middle English period, but that these dialects also went on to contribute much of their lexicon to Standard English. By contrast, French loans found in Northern dialects tend to have remained dialectal: examples are *howlet* for 'owl', *poke* for 'sack', *rammel* for 'rubbish', *ratten* for 'rat' and *scallions* for 'spring onions'. The last of these is also found in small enclaves in the South, which might suggest that it was formerly more widespread. As we shall see in Section 4.3, Northern dialects are often more conservative than those of the South-East, so, in this case, a dialectal French loan may have been ousted by the Standard English *spring onions* earlier in most of the South.

Another reason for the presence of French words in Northern dialects could be contact or continuity with Scots. Words not included in Orton and Wright, such as *ashet*, 'serving plate', *fash* 'bother' and *douse* 'pleasant', are recorded in Wright's *English Dialect Dictionary* (*EDD*, 1898–1905) as occurring in Scotland and also in Northern counties such as Northumberland, Cumberland and parts of Yorkshire. Wright's entry for *ashet* includes a comment from the Northumbrian dialectologist R. O. Heslop that the word is 'heard on the n. borders, but not in gen. use, and prob. introduced by immigrants from Scotland' (1898–1905: 80).

4.2.3 Words of Dutch and Low German origin

There has been considerable contact between speakers of English and of Low German dialects, the latter mainly from what are now Belgium and the Netherlands. Craftsmen from these areas brought specialised skills to many areas of England, whilst others came here as refugees. According to Orton and Wright (1974: 30) words from this source 'are not confined to a particular region, but occur in separate enclaves variously distributed'. Orton and Wright also point out that Low German is so similar to Old and Middle English that we cannot always be sure whether words are native or borrowed.

Some words of Dutch origin are found mainly in the East of the country, as we might expect given the sea-routes that still exist between these two areas. Examples are *haar* 'sea-fog', found (according to *EDD*) in Northumberland, Durham, Yorkshire, Lincolnshire and Lancashire; and *ploat* 'to pluck (a fowl)', confined to Northumberland, Durham, North Yorkshire and the eastern parts of Cumberland and Westmoreland (according to SED). *Snap* 'mid-morning snack' is found in SED in parts of South Yorkshire, Derbyshire, Nottinghamshire, Staffordshire and Leicestershire. Orton and Wright refer to this geographical distribution as 'the heart of the ncMidl' ([North Central Midlands] 1974: 31), but what is significant about this area is that much of it had extensive coalfields, where *snap* is the term used by miners to refer to the meal taken down the mine with them. In Peter Wright's (1972) study of coal-mining language, *snap* is the word used for 'the food you take to work with you for a meal' in all the locations he studied in Yorkshire, plus those in Nottinghamshire, Shropshire, Lancashire and South Wales. Indeed, it is the most widely diffused term for this notion, used in seven out of fifteen locations: no other term is used in more than one location. It is unlikely that this use of the word was introduced by Dutch or Flemish miners, since, according to *EDD*, it was more widespread in England and Scotland as a verb meaning 'to eat hastily' or as a noun meaning 'a small portion of food, a hasty meal', and, of course, *snap* with meanings related to biting is found in StE. So *snap* was probably borrowed in English with the sense 'a quick or sudden closing of the jaws or teeth in biting' and the semantic development as a word for 'packed lunch' came later. It is cited as a specific mining term in Gresley's coal-mining glossary of 1883 and was probably diffused through these coalfields by miners and retained in these areas. This demonstrates that we should not assume direct language contact whenever a word with a 'foreign' etymology is found in a specific dialect area.

On the other hand, there is certainly evidence in some areas of England for settlements of Dutch and/or Flemish speakers leaving their mark on the dialect vocabulary. In the sixteenth century, craftsmen from what is now Belgium were invited to settle in Norwich in order to modernise the textile industry, and later in the century, when the Low Countries came under Spanish control, these settlers were joined by refugees fleeing religious persecution at the hands of the Inquisition. These included French-speaking Walloons as well as speakers of Dutch/Flemish. Trudgill tells us that 'by 1579, 37% of the population of Norwich ... were native speakers of Dutch or French' and that Norwich 'remained a trilingual city ... well into the 18th century' (2003: 28–9). Trudgill, like Wright and Orton, notes that it is not always possible to state definitively that words come from Dutch rather than Old English, but suggests that *dwile* 'floorcloth', *crowd* 'to push a wheelbarrow or bicycle' and *push* 'boil, pimple' are probably from Dutch or Flemish (2003: 38).

4.2.4 Words of Celtic origin

Histories and dictionaries of English tend to be very cautious about attributing Celtic etymologies to words in both Standard English and regional dialects: Filppula et al. note that historians of English have 'somewhat grudgingly … admitted the possibility of Celtic influence in the Old and Middle English periods' (2002: 20). Orton and Wright include 'only three words of undoubted Celtic origin' (1974: 32), and all of these are located in or on the borders of areas where Celtic languages survived longest. *Car-* and *clicky-*, both compounded with *-handed* to mean 'left-handed', are found in Northern Northumberland and Corn- wall/West Dorset respectively. *Car* is derived from Gaelic *cearr*, and its extreme northerly distribution in England suggests it has entered from Scotland, whilst *clicky* is from Cornish. The other 'Celtic' word in Orton and Wright is *tallet* 'hay-loft', derived from Welsh *taflod*, and this, as we might expect, is found in the English counties on the Welsh border, but also in much of the South-West.

Fischer in his lexical study of South-Western dialects finds a few more Celtic words: *pig's-crow* 'pigsty', *bucca* 'scarecrow', *dram* 'swath', (*piggy*)- *whidden* 'runt, weakling' and 'perhaps' *clunker* 'windpipe'. He is less certain that *clicky-(handed)* is Cornish, and suggests *butt* 'skep' 'may be Cornish', but notes that 'these cases are still open to discussion' (1976: 304). In addition to *tallet*, he also found, *tump* 'clamp' and *cam-*(handed), yet another word for 'left-handed', all from Welsh, and he suggests that *bodkin* 'swingle-tree' may also be from this source. This seems to be very meagre evidence from a 'Celtic' area, but Fischer admits that 'the material here is incomplete with regard to the Cornish element in south-western dialects' (1976: 304).

Wakelin (1977: 128–9) has a more extensive list of Cornish words in the English dialect of West Cornwall, including *bannell* 'broom', *fuggan* 'pastry dinner-cake', *gook* 'bonnet', *griglans* 'heather', *groushans* 'dregs', *gurgoe* 'warren', *hoggan* 'pastry cake', *kewny* 'rancid', *muryans* 'ants', *padgy- pow* 'newt', *rab* 'gravel', *scaw* 'elder tree', *stank* 'to walk, trample, step (on, in)' and *tidden* 'tender'.

As we saw in Chapter 3, nineteenth-century migration from Ireland to urban centres, especially in the North of England, may have had some influence on the urban dialects, plural *yous(e)* being a case in point. It would be tempting to see *crack*, meaning 'talk, conversation, gossip' and found, according to EDD, in all the Northern counties as well as Scotland, as deriving from Irish *craic*. However, the story is more com- plicated: *crack* is found in Northern English dialects before the period of Irish immigration, and Irish *craic* is, according to Dolan (1998), a word borrowed into Irish from English. It is possible that the Irish-English sense of 'fun' has influenced the use of the word in recent times, but this might be due more to the marketing strategies of Irish brewers than to immigration. Another Northern English dialect word with a possible Celtic etymology is *gob* 'mouth'. In the SED, this is found in parts of Northumberland, Durham, Westmoreland, Cumberland, Lancashire and parts of Derbyshire, Yorkshire, Lincolnshire and Norfolk. It is listed here as 'orig. obsc.', but the Irish word *gob* also refers to the mouth. The OED, whilst marking it as of 'obscure origin', concedes that it is 'possibly a. Gael. and Irish *gob* beak, mouth'. However, Roper (2004) suggests that a Norse etymology is also possible and points out the 'Scandinavian Belt' nature of the word's geographical distribution in traditional dialects.

4.2.5 Words of Romani/Angloromani origin

Scandinavian, French, Dutch and Celtic are the major sources of 'borrowed' words in English regional dialects, and the only ones discussed in Orton and Wright (1974). However, other languages have come into contact with vernacular forms of English and left their mark. Often, these sources have been ignored in accounts of traditional dialects because they have tended to affect urban dialects, or because they have no clear geographical pattern and are therefore perceived as 'slang'. Words from Romani are a case in point: this is the language of the Romany, and words from this source are found in traditional dialects in areas on established travelling routes and/or with traditional fairs and markets. Angloromani is the term used for an English dialect used by travellers which includes Romani vocabulary. This has influenced the language of market traders in large cities, so words from this source are also found in urban dialects.

The distribution of a set of words all derived from Romani *čhavo* meaning 'unmarried male' or 'male child' illustrates this. *Chavvy* is cited in the *OED* as 'British slang (originally cant)' and as coming from Angloromani *chavvy* 'child'. The citations are from Scots and from Cockney, the latter mainly from representations of market traders and criminals in the media, such as the following:

> **1989** J. SULLIVAN *Only Fools & Horses* (2000) II. 6th Ser. Episode 6. 127/2 Marlene's pregnancy is costing me an arm and a leg. She's at a dodgy age for knocking out her first chavvy.

Charver, which has the same etymology, is defined in the *OED* as 'a young person of a type characterized by brash and loutish behaviour and the wearing of designer-style clothes (esp. sportswear); usually with connotations of a low social status' and designated as 'Engl. regional (north-east). slang'. All the citations are recent (the earliest 1997) and all from sources in Newcastle upon Tyne. Perhaps the most widely recognised word in this set is *chav*. The *OED* designates this as 'British slang (usually derogatory)' and gives a definition identical to that for *charver*, except that it is prefaced by 'In the United Kingdom (originally the south of England)'. This word was taken up by the media in the early twenty-first century and so spread from the South (folk-etymology associates it with Chatham in Kent) throughout Britain. As we shall see in Section 4.4, distinctions between 'dialect' and 'slang' are not always easy to make, and words which have a regional origin may become more widespread. Moreover, regional words may be used alongside national 'slang' by speakers who are unaware of the distinctions imposed on these words by linguists.

On the 'BBC Voices' website, Yaron Matras points out that 'the border area between Scotland and England was a favourite area of settle-ment' and that 'many local dialects in Northumbria have incorporated words of Romani origin into the local slang' (www.bbc.co.uk/voices/multilingual/romani_history.shtml#A). In addition to *charver*, discussed above, *gadgie*, used to mean 'old man' in Tyneside and Northumberland, comes from *gaujo*, meaning 'a non-Romany'. *Cushty*, shortened to *cush* by younger speakers on Tyneside, means 'good, wonderful' and can be traced to Romani *kushto/kushti*. This word is also found in London, and was popularised and spread throughout Britain by the TV series *Only Fools and Horses*, a source also cited by the *OED* for *chavvy*.

4.3 Retention in English dialects

We saw in Section 4.2.1 that, whereas the Scandinavian word *beck* is found in dialects within the 'Scandinavian Belt', to the north and south of this area the words *burn* and *brook* are used respectively. Both the latter terms come from Old English sources, but it is another Old English word, *stream*, that has become the Standard English term for this concept. Much of the lexicon of English dialects is made up of Old English words that were formerly more widespread, but have been retained only in specific areas, having been ousted from other regional dialects and from Standard English by competing synonyms. Examples of this are *brambles*, an Old English word used in the North-East and Lincolnshire, whilst *blackberries* (also Old English) is found elsewhere and in Standard English; *ask*, found in the far North, Lancashire and the counties bordering Wales, synonymous with *newt* in other dialects and in

Standard English; and *naught/somewhat*, compared to Standard English *nothing/something*.

Of course, both *naught* and *somewhat* are still used in Standard English, but with different meanings and different pronunciations. *Naught* means 'zero' and is pronounced /nɔːt/ in StE, whilst *somewhat* means 'rather' and is pronounced /sʌmwɒt/ in StE. In Northern dialects, these are pronounced /naʊt/ or /nɛʊt/ and /sʊmət/ respectively, would be spelled <nowt> and <summat> in dialect literature, and are perceived as lexically distinct from the Standard English *nought, somewhat*. In my own dialect (South Lancashire/North Cheshire), / nɛʊt / <nowt> and /nɔːt/ <nought> are perceived as two different words, the former meaning either 'nothing' or 'a naughty child', the latter meaning 'zero'. On Tyneside, I have heard *nothing* used to mean the figure zero when a telephone number was given, because in this dialect *nowt* would indicate that there was no number there.

Bairn, found in the North-East, Cumbria and Lincolnshire in the SED, has sometimes been given a Scandinavian etymology (cf. modern Norwegian *barn*), and its geographical distribution would support this, but it could equally well be descended from Old English *beorn* since the word was formerly more widespread and was ousted in the South and in Standard English by Old English *child*.

In other cases of retention, a loan-word has replaced the Old English word in Standard English and in the majority of dialects. For example, *till* from Old Norse, is used in most of the country and in StE to complete the sentence 'wait … the sun goes down', but in much of Yorkshire and parts of Lancashire, Lincolnshire and Nottinghamshire the Old English *while* is used. This usage is still very widespread in these areas, and is not perceived as non-standard: notices on Sheffield shop doors advertising opening hours as, for instance, '9 while 5' are by no means rare.

We saw in Chapters 2 and 3 that 'relict' features, such as rhoticity in pronunciation and pronoun exchange in grammar, are characteristic of regional accents and dialects, and so it is not surprising that the same patterns are found in lexis. In the next section, we will consider the extent to which these 'old' words are still used and the ways in which speakers use these more 'traditional' dialect words in variation with newer ones.

4.4 Variation and change in regional lexis

4.4.1 Retention and loss of dialect words

Although, as we noted in Section 4.1, the study of variation and change in lexis has been neglected in comparison to that of phonology and morphology/syntax, there have been some attempts to compare the SED findings with those from later surveys in order to gauge the extent of the loss of regional diversity in vocabulary. Upton and Widdowson, commenting on the Northern distribution of *oxter* for 'armpit', suggest:

> It would be most interesting to investigate the present-day survival of such words as this, words which have been strongly supported by dialect speakers in a well-defined area but which have been little known in the country at large. (1996: 83)

Prompted by this, Simmelbauer (2000) carried out a survey of lexical usage in Northumberland. She compiled a questionnaire designed to elicit 101 concepts for which either the SED materials or other sources such as dialect dictionaries had a word which was local to Northumberland, and interviewed subjects of both genders and three age-groups in eleven localities from Newcastle in the south to Tweedmouth in the far north of the county (before the 1974 administrative reorganisation, which changed county boundaries). She found that some 'traditional' dialect words were still widely known, several were known by very few or no subjects, and knowledge of others varied according to the age and/or gender and/or location of the informants. The most widely known words, elicited from more than 50 per cent of subjects in all localities and 100 per cent in some, were (in order) *bait* 'packed meal', *fettle* 'mood', *lugs* 'ears', *spelk* 'splinter', *gob* 'mouth', *bramble* 'blackberry', *claggy* 'sticky', *grub* 'food', *hoy* 'throw' and *burn* 'rivulet'. The ten least-known words, ranging from 0 per cent to 20 per cent in all localities, were *flaycrow* 'scarecrow', *whangs* 'shoelaces', *ruddick* 'robin', *booly* 'broken earthenware', *pissiemoor* 'ant', *tanklet* 'icicle', *gowk* 'cuckoo', *steg* 'gander', *blushes* 'blisters' and *whicker* 'to whinny'. Where there was variation between subjects' knowledge of words, Simmelbauer found that the most significant factor was age: 'the use and knowledge of dialect words decreases with decreasing age' (2000: 239). This suggests that some dialect words are being lost, but the 100 per cent scores for others demonstrate that these are more resilient. Simmelbauer found that females tended to know more or less the same number of dialect words as males, and, with regard to location, that 'smaller localities in rural areas ... have preserved more dialect words than larger communities, which have changed more rapidly over the last decades' (2000: 239).

In a paper dealing with the issue of 'dialect death'more generally, Britain (2009) comments on a survey carried out by the Norwich-based *Eastern Daily Press* in 1991. A list of 'local' dialect words was distributed across the region to adults and children, who were asked whether they recognised the words. Britain reports that 'the rate of lexical attrition is considerable and dramatic, with those over 60 recognizing over three-quarters of the words, and those under 18 less than one word in five' (2009: 124). Britain then investigated which words were most likely to have been lost and found that words such as *harnser* (heron) and *planchard* (a boarded floor), which were restricted to Norfolk and Suffolk even in Wright's *English Dialect Dictionary* (1898–1905), 'were less than half as likely to be recognized by adults and *fourteen* times less likely by the under 18-year-olds as those found beyond East Anglia' (2009: 125, emphasis in original).

Simmelbauer's study and Britain's brief report both show that studies of variation and change in lexis can be informative. Whilst Simmelbauer's research was confined to a specific county, Upton and Widdowson (1999) carried out a nationwide study. They aimed to determine the extent of 'lexical erosion' in English dialects by comparing the range of words for specific notions elicited by the SED with those collected in England for the lexical section of the Atlas Linguarum Europae (ALE) project. The latter survey was conducted between 1976 and 1980 in sixty-six localities which had all been included in the SED's network. Since ALE, like the SED, collected data from older informants in rural locations, Upton and Widdowson were able to make direct comparisons between the two surveys in a real-time study of lexical change.

Upton and Widdowson's results are divided into four categories, or 'tiers': A (forty-seven records), where no comparison was possible; B (fifty-four records), where ALE recorded more variants than SED; C (seventy records), where SED recorded more variants than ALE; and D (sixty-eight records), where SED and ALE recorded an equal number of variants. Whether these results constitute evidence of 'lexical erosion' is debatable: although there are more records in category C (ALE < SED, demonstrating loss) than in category B (ALE > SED, demonstrating gain), the number in category D (ALE = SED, demonstrating stability) is almost as great as that in category C. An optimist could conclude that, since the sum of B + D is greater than C, there is no proof of overall erosion of regional variability in the lexicon of English. Upton and Widdowson take the more pessimistic view, concluding that 'there is no doubt that the regional dialect lexicon is being eroded, and across its full range rather than simply in the more specialised fields of usage' (1999: 22). They see the evidence for erosion as more compelling because many of the 'new' words elicited by ALE are 'slang or standard words as distinct from "traditional" dialect' (1999: 22). Examples of these tendencies are *abdomen* for 'belly', *casket* for 'coffin', *forge* for 'anvil', *offspring* for 'children' (all standard), and *spondulicks* for 'money' and *ton* for 'hundred', both 'slang'. As we shall see in the next section, the distinction between 'dialect' and 'slang' is often neither understood nor observed by participants in recent surveys of lexical variation.

4.4.2 Variation and innovation in regional lexis

The studies discussed in Section 4.4.1 suggest that the vocabulary of regional English is being 'levelled' as some traditional dialect words cease to be used or known in areas where they had formerly been recorded (Simmelbauer 2000), and the diversity of terms formerly recorded in national surveys is lessened (Upton and Widdowson 1999). However, Simmelbauer also notes 'some dialect words' which are 'frequently elicited from the youngest interviewees while the elderly report hardly any instances' and suggests that 'this development could be seen as a sign of innovation' (2000: 207). This would indicate that the 'erosion' noted by Upton and Widdowson is only one side of the story where lexical variation and change are concerned and that, just as in phonology and morphology/syntax, there are regional patterns of innovation as well as loss. The problem is that, where vocabulary is concerned, innovations tend to be classified as 'slang' rather than 'dialect'. After noting the innovatory usage of her younger subjects, Simmelbauer goes on to state that these words 'can hardly ever be classed as traditional dialect words, but rather as non-standard terms which are also found in other British dialects' (2000: 207).

We noted in Section 4.2.5 that the *OED* describes the word *charver* as 'Engl. regional (north-east). slang'. Note here the full stop before 'slang', indicating that the word is both 'regional'- the term now used by the OED in place of former 'dial.' (Philip Durkin, personal communication) – and 'slang'. In her historical study of slang dictionaries, Coleman defines *slang* as follows:

> *Slang* terms are characteristically short-lived, and tend to be used by a closed group of people, often united by common interests. Each generation has its own slang of approval and disapproval. (2004: 4)

This suggests that words associated with a particular time or generation would be classified as 'slang', but this becomes problematic when applied to innovations, for how can we know in advance which words used by young people will stand the test of time? Two recent studies have shown that, if we consider the full range of lexical variants used for concepts today, regional patterns can still be found and the loss of diversity noted by Upton and Widdowson (1999) is not apparent. These studies both make use of an innovative method of data collection known as the

Sense Relation Network Sheet (SRN), an example of which is shown in Figure 4.3.

Carmen Llamas, under the supervision of Clive Upton and John Widdowson at the Universities of Leeds and Sheffield respectively, devised this methodology using Aitchison's (1997: 61) notion of the 'web of words'. Instead of eliciting single-word responses as SED-type questionnaires do, the SRN encourages subjects to record all the words they know and/or use for a network of interrelated concepts. This tends to result in a wide range of terms being elicited, which are then discussed in a recorded interview. Llamas applied this methodology to a study of variation and change in Teesside English, and found that speakers were not always aware which of the words they used were 'dialectal'. She cites the example of an informant who 'claimed not to have inserted a variant for *soft shoes worn by children for P.E.* because she "couldn't think of another word for *sandshoes*"' (Llamas 1999: 113). This indicates that the informant considers *sandshoes* to be the Standard English term whereas it is, in fact, regionally restricted within England to the North-East, as can be seen in Trudgill (1994: 22–4).

Using SRNs allows the researcher to discover the full extent of lexical variation, without excluding words on the grounds that they are not 'dialectal'. The SRN was initially developed as a tool for a projected Survey of Regional English (Kerswill et al. 1999), but it has since been modified for use by the BBC Voices project, in which fifty journalists from local radio stations throughout the UK were trained to administer SRNs to groups of speakers in their areas. Some of the data from this project can be found at www.bbc.co.uk/voices. The project also encouraged members of the public to send in responses to their 'word maps', results from which can be found on the same website. The data presented by the BBC Voices project belies the suggestion that lexical diversity is being eroded. For the concept THROW, Upton and Widdowson (1996: 179) note that thirty-four different words were recorded by the SED. Far from showing 'levelling' to a narrower range of variants, the BBC Voices website records forty-five words, some of which were not recorded in the SED. Although *chuck* was the most widely used term, some words, notably *hoy* and *cob*, were regionally distributed.

Another example of the range of regional variants used for a single concept is that of the words for a 'young person in cheap trendy clothes and jewellery'. A total of fifty-seven words were submitted, and, whilst the most widely distributed term was *chav*, others showed a more regional distribution, notably *ned* in Scotland, *charva* in the North-East and *pikey* in the South. Both these cases demonstrate that, whilst a single word may be known nationwide, it will often be used alongside more

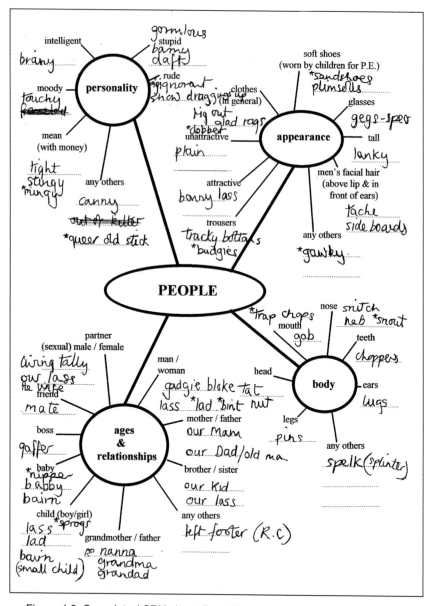

Figure 4.3 Completed SRN sheet (from Llamas 1999: 114).

regionally restricted words for the same concept, some of which are 'traditional' dialect words and others innovative terms which might well be dismissed as 'slang' by less inclusive studies.

In order to determine the full extent and nature of regional lexical variation in twenty-first-century English, we need to record all the words known and used for a range of concepts and to find out who uses these words and in what contexts. Llamas was able to elicit this kind of information in her interviews: she tells us of 'two young male Middlesbrough informants arguing that they would never use the variant *bonny* for the notion word "attractive", it being "an old person's word", and that they would never use *canny-looking*, it being used by girls, opting themselves to use *nectar, sweet, fit* and *lush*' (1999: 104).

A case in point is the use of the Northern terms *lad* and *lass*, for Standard English *boy/girl* and/or *son/daughter*. Glauser (1985) analysed the geographical distribution of lexical variants in these semantic fields in the SED material. He found that *lad* was 'used almost exclusively north of a line running from southern Shropshire to the Wash' and, whilst there were more variants for GIRL/DAUGHTER, *lass* was 'still mainly confined to the North'. He also found that *lad* was used more frequently than *lass*. 'Combinations of LAD/GIRL are much more common than LASS/BOY'.

Glauser's research confirms that both *lad* and *lass* are regional (Northern), but the SED data give no information about how these terms were actually used by the informants and whether they would vary with Standard English and/or other words. Opportunities for investigating lexical variation in use are now provided by the corpora of regional varieties of English which are now becoming available. The NECTE corpus provides transcripts of interviews and conversations recorded in 1969 and 1994 respectively, in which we can see standard and regional variants being used. The evidence suggests that both *lad* and *lass* are still used by young people, and that these words vary with both the Standard English terms *boy/girl* and slang terms such as *bloke/guy*. Amongst adolescents recorded in 1994 *lad* and *lass* are often used to refer to peers, especially friends or potential boyfriends/girlfriends. Informant PVC1b, a young man between 16 and 20 years old at the time of recording, regularly refers to his girlfriend as *wor lass*, as in the following two extracts:

So I ended up sticking to the southern comforts all night. Wor lass gans 'oh you're not going to drink too much of that are you?'

Wor lass was drinking purple passions all night oh they were gorgeous.

His friend (PVC1a), however, refers to his own partner with the SE term *girlfriend*.

Going to the girlfriend's concert first though

I don't even know my girlfriend's birthday

Elsewhere in this conversation, both refer to young women of their own age as *lasses*. In all, the word *lass* is used eleven times in the interview as against four instances of *girl (friend)*. *Lad* is much more frequent than *boy*, the latter only used once in *boyfriend*. It would seem that, for these two young, lower-middle-class Tynesiders, *lad* and *lass* are the normal terms for males and females of their own age. Older men are always referred to as *blokes* in this conversation: Standard English *man* is used only as a generic term, as in 'it's a man's watch'.

A conversation between two young women from the same corpus also demonstrates that both *lad* and *lass* are the normal terms for young men and women. These two young women discuss gender issues and so both *man* and *woman* are used generically:

I-mean man can do a woman's job, and a woman can do a man's job (PVCL2)

However, where males and females of their own age are referred to, both these young women regularly use *lad* and *lass*.

Is it just all lasses, or do lads go? (PVC/L2)

They say lads are a lot better to work with than with lasses you know (PVCK1)

This is just a brief snapshot of the way in which the regional words *lad* and *lass* are used by young Tynesiders, but the examples provided above are sufficient to demonstrate that knowledge and use of Standard English and/or 'slang' variants do not necessarily mean that more traditional, regional variants are abandoned.

4.5 Summary

In this chapter, I have shown how lexical variation in English regional dialects reflects historical patterns of contact with speakers of other languages. Whilst these early contacts have provided what are generally agreed to be 'traditional' dialect terms, words introduced in recent times have tended to be viewed as 'slang' and as constituting a threat to the traditional dialect vocabulary. However, evidence from recent surveys such as BBC Voices suggests that speakers often incorporate newer terms as variants rather than abandoning the traditional ones altogether, a picture which is confirmed by the examination of actual usage in corpora. Nevertheless, much more research is needed before we can know to what extent regional variation in the vocabulary of English is indeed being reduced, and whether Upton and Widdowson (1999: 10) are right in seeing this process of lexical erosion as parallel to the levelling observed in the areas of phonology and morphosyntax. In the next chapter, I shall discuss more generally the evidence for levelling and diffusion in English dialects.

Exercises

- Using the Sense Relation Network Sheet on page 72, write down all the words you know for the concepts written on one of the sections ('being', 'saying' or 'doing'). Take time over this, as you will not think of all the words you know right away.
- Compare the words you have listed with those listed by others in your class. Are there differences between males and females or between people from different places?
- Which of the words that you have listed would you consider to be slang and which do you think are dialect words, and why?
- Look up some of the words in the online *Oxford English Dictionary* (www.oed.com) and find out (i) their origins and (ii) where they are used.

Further reading

There have been comparatively few studies of lexical variation in dialects of English. Orton and Wright (1974) provides a historical introduction and a large range of maps based on material from the SED. A more accessible SED-based atlas is Upton and Widdowson (1996). Upton et al. (1994) presents the material from the SED in the form of a dictionary. Simmelbauer (2002) is a study of lexical change in the Northumbrian dialect, and Upton and Widdowson (1999) is a more general survey of lexical erosion in British English dialects.

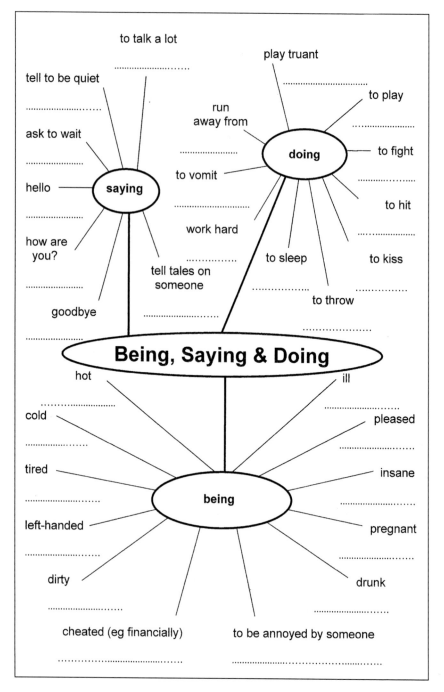

5 Levelling and diffusion

5.1 Introduction

This book began with an account of the perceived loss of regionally distinct dialects, both now and in the past. Chapters 2, 3 and 4 have contained references to research providing evidence of levelling in the phonology, grammar and lexis of English dialects respectively. In this chapter, I first examine the processes which lead to levelling and then present the results of recent research which casts doubt on the notion that English dialects are becoming less distinct from each other.

Kerswill (2003: 223), whilst referring to 'regional dialect levelling ... leading to the loss of localised features', distinguishes two separate 'mechanisms behind these changes': *geographical diffusion* and *levelling*. The first of these is defined as a process 'by which features spread out from a populous and economically and culturally dominant centre' (2003: 223). Changes involving diffusion have an identifiable historical starting-point and geographical trajectory: 'new' variants can be seen to have spread or to be spreading, displacing 'old' variants indigenous to the places affected. By contrast, the process of levelling, defined by Trudgill as involving 'the reduction or attrition of *marked* variants' (1986: 98, emphasis in original), occurs when speakers of different dialects come into contact. These speakers, and hence the variants brought in by them, could have a diversity of origins, but in the contact situation, variants which are more 'local' and/or less widespread tend to be discarded. 'The outcome is the levelling of differences among what was at first a conglomeration of varieties, often leading to a new variety characterised by the absence of localised forms' (Kerswill 2003: 223). Kerswill points out that there is an 'awkward terminological ambiguity' (2003: 224) in that 'levelling' is used to refer both to the general effect of loss of local distinctiveness, and to one of the processes that brings this about. In the next two sections, I discuss each of these two mechanisms in turn, along with the evidence for their operation in late twentieth- and early twenty-first-century England.

5.2 Levelling

In situations where speakers of different varieties come into contact, levelling occurs as a result of a process known as accommodation. This process was described by Giles and Powesland (1975), who found that speakers shifted their accents to be more similar to interlocutors whom they valued positively and to be more dissimilar to those they valued negatively. The former process is known as convergence, and the latter divergence. In a situation of long-term dialect contact, frequent acts of convergence and divergence might eventually lead to long-term accommodation (see Kerswill 2003: 223; Trudgill 1986: 1–38). In this process, convergence would lead to the dominance of majority and/or prestige variants, whilst divergence would involve the avoidance of variants which are rarer and/or negatively valued. Either way, the end result would be the loss of minority variants and hence levelling.

Although, as discussed in Chapter 1, concerns about loss of dialectal distinctiveness are by no means new, dialect levelling is a phenomenon which has been given a great deal of attention by sociolinguists in the late twentieth and early twenty-first centuries. This is probably because the social conditions which lead to levelling have been operating on a much bigger scale in recent times. Migration of populations to urban centres is nothing new: Nevalainen and Raumolin-Brunberg (2003) demonstrate that migration to London led to levelling in Early Modern English, and the nineteenth-century dialectologists cited in Chapter 1 of this book express concern about the likely levelling effect of migration to industrial centres. However, in recent times, mobility has become the norm for a much higher proportion of the population of England. The creation of New Towns, initially to ease the housing shortage after World War II, led to the mixing of people from various parts of the country in these locations, and, more recently, government intervention to regenerate former industrial areas, particularly in the North, has provided incentives for organisations and their employees to relocate to these areas. The expansion of higher education in the late twentieth century means that a high proportion of young adults, especially those from middle-class backgrounds, are educated at universities distant from their birthplace and/or relocate several times in their lifetime to find employment. Even those who do not relocate may commute to work, and so come into daily contact with speakers of other varieties. There are thus many more opportunities for dialect contact for a much higher proportion of the population than in earlier periods, though it needs to be recognised that there are still sections of the population, such as the long-term unemployed, whose opportunities for geographical (and social) mobility are severely restricted. I shall now go on to consider two studies of phonological dialect levelling in England, one in a New Town and the other in a post-industrial Northern city, before looking at some evidence for morphological and syntactic levelling.

Kerswill and Williams carried out a study in Milton Keynes, one of the 'third wave' of New Towns created in the 1960s (see Kerswill and Williams 2000: 76–7 for a historical account of the three waves of New Town building in Britain). Although a latecomer compared to New Towns of the first wave such as Stevenage, Milton Keynes has entered English folklore as the prototypical 'soulless' New Town (Finnegan 1998). It was designated a New Town in 1967, and initially took most of its population from London and the South-East of England, although more recent in-migration has been mainly from the surrounding counties of Buckinghamshire, Bedfordshire and Northamptonshire (Kerswill and Williams 2000: 14). Kerswill and Williams used a sample of forty-eight children either born in Milton Keynes or having moved there within the first two years of their lives, divided into equal groups of boys and girls aged 4, 8 and 12. The researchers also recorded the speech of the children's main caregiver, in most cases the mother, along with six elderly residents who had lived all their lives in the area. The speech of these elderly residents, together with evidence from the nearest SED location, Stewksley, was used as evidence for the traditional dialect of the Milton Keynes area. What Kerswill and Williams found was that, with regard to a range of vocalic and consonantal features, the variability found in the older generation was giving way to a more 'focused', homogeneous variety in the second generation. In this 'new dialect', both traditional variants local to the Milton Keynes area and some London English variants were found to have been discarded by the younger generation, who instead 'seemed to be settling on compromise variants that were phonetically intermediate between London English and RP' (Kerswill and Williams 2000: 96).

Kerswill and Williams also noted that the patterns of variation and change in Milton Keynes were similar to those found elsewhere in the South of England, pointing to dialect levelling over a wider area. An example of this is the distribution of variants of MOUTH. Elderly speakers in both Milton Keynes and Reading used the traditional variants [ɛʏ] and [ɛɪ] but adolescents predominantly used [aʊ]. The difference between the two sets of speakers was that, whilst in Reading some tokens of the traditional variants were found in the speech of adolescent boys, they were totally absent from the speech of Milton Keynes adolescents. Kerswill and Williams suggest that Milton Keynes is 'ahead' of Reading in this shift away from traditional variants because, as a New Town, it lacks Reading's close-knit social networks, which are associated with linguistic conservatism (Milroy and Milroy 1982).

Kerswill and Williams point out that 'Milton Keynes lies in an already extensively leveled [sic] dialect area' (2000: 80), i.e. the South-East of England, but evidence of dialect levelling has also been found in other parts of the country. Watt and Milroy (1999) present evidence from Newcastle upon Tyne, the most northerly city in England. In this variety, there are three main variants of FACE and four of GOAT, as set out in Figure 5.1.

FACE	GOAT
eː	oː
ɪə	ʊə
eɪ	oʊ
	øː

Figure 5.1 Variants of FACE and GOAT in Newcastle (after Watt and Milroy 1999).

The 'local' variants here are the centring diphthongs [ɪə] and [ʊə]. In the case of FACE, the group of speakers who use the centring diphthong variants more than any of the others is that of the older, working-class men. Watt and Milroy point out that use of this variant 'becomes less frequent as a function of age … and class' but that 'gender is the variable which divides the speakers most sharply, as female speakers use centring diphthong variants very rarely' (1999: 35). For all groups except the older, working-class males, there is a clear preference for what Watt and Milroy term the 'unmarked' variant, the monophthong [eː]. The third variant, the closing diphthong [eɪ], is used very infrequently, and only by younger middle-class speakers (male and female).

With regard to GOAT, a similar pattern emerged, albeit complicated by the presence of a fourth variant. Here again, there was a 'preference for the unmarked variant [oː] by all groups except the WC [working-class] males' (Watt and Milroy 1999: 36). In this case, older, working-class males were found to use the variants [ʊə], [oː] and [øː] in approximately equal proportions. As was the case with FACE, the centring diphthong was avoided by women and was most frequent in the speech of older, working-class men, whilst the closing diphthong was very infrequent overall, but used mainly by younger, middle-class speakers. The fourth variant [øː] was used much more by men than by women, but younger, middle-class men were using it more than older, working-class men.

Comparing the results for FACE and GOAT, Watt and Milroy conclude that the majority of their sample, especially females, younger and middle-class speakers, most frequently use what they term the 'unmarked northern mainstream monophthongal FACE and GOAT variants [e:] and [o:]' (1999: 40). The researchers note that these monophthongal pronunciations are found in a wide range of Northern accents, whilst the centring diphthongs are very localised and therefore 'marked'. They conclude that 'the salient pattern of change is a reduction in variability across two generations; localised variants either disappear or are reduced in number and younger speakers prefer mainstream, unmarked variants' (1999: 41). This move towards 'unmarked' variants fits the definition of levelling set out at the beginning of this chapter. However, Watt and Milroy point out that this is not a case of levelling to a national norm, but to a 'supra-local' pan-Northern variety, perhaps parallel to the Southern 'Estuary English'. In both cases, the social forces behind the levelling are the same: disruption of traditional, close-knit networks by geographical mobility and subsequent contact between speakers of different varieties.

Watt (1998) suggests that issues of identity may also play a part in the levelling of Tyneside English. He argues that the shift is most advanced amongst younger speakers, who want to retain their local/regional identity, but do not want to be associated with the old-fashioned 'cloth-cap-and-clogs' image of their parents. The very noticeably 'Geordie' features are lost, but are replaced by 'Northern' ones, so that they 'sound like northerners, but *modern* northerners' (1998: 7). We will return to this point in the next chapter.

Although most of the research into levelling in English dialects has dealt with phonological features, levelling is not confined to accent. Cheshire et al. (1993) discuss the widespread distribution of a range of non-standard grammatical features throughout urban areas of Britain. They found that the non-standard grammatical features listed below were reported throughout Britain:

- demonstrative *them* ('look at *them* spiders')
- *should of*
- absence of plural marking ('you need *two pound* of flour')
- *what* as subject relative pronoun ('the film *what* was on last night')
- *never* as past tense negator ('No, I *never* broke that')
- *there was/there's* with plural subject ('*There was* some singers here a minute ago'; '*There's* cars outside the church')
- perfect participle *sat/stood* following *be* ('She was *sat/stood* over there looking at her car')
- adverbial *quick* ('I like pasta. It cooks real *quick*')
- *ain't/in't* ('That *ain't/in't* working')

- *give me it*
- non-standard *was* ('We *was* singing')

In some cases, the researchers noted a reduction of variation, especially in inner-city areas as opposed to suburbs, smaller towns and rural areas. For instance, a wider range of non-standard demonstratives, including *this here* and *that there*, was reported outside the city area of Manchester, whereas within the city only *them* was reported. Since the population of the inner cities would tend to be more heterogeneous, this could constitute evidence of dialect levelling

5.3 Diffusion

5.3.1 Patterns of diffusion

We saw in Section 5.1 that the mechanism of diffusion is distinguished from that of levelling in that the former involves the spread of an innovating feature *from* a specific locality, whilst the latter requires dialect contact *within* a locality. Kerswill suggests that levelling takes place 'in cases where there is high mobility within a relatively compact area' and that, where innovations spread over a much wider area, such as the whole of Britain, 'geographical diffusion is the more likely mechanism' (2003: 240). Diffusion need not necessarily involve long-term contact: a variant can 'spread' as a result of casual contact, which can involve travelling to a larger town or city for leisure, shopping or commuting. Where features of dialect rather than accent are concerned, contact resulting in diffusion can take place via the media and electronic communication.

Britain provides a list of four different patterns of diffusion that have been noted by researchers:

- *'wave'* or *'contagion'* diffusion ..., whereby innovations, over time, radiate out from a central focal area, reaching physically nearby locations before those at ever greater distances;
- *'urban hierarchical'* diffusion ..., whereby innovations descend down a scale of hierarchy of large city to city to large town, to town, village and country;
- *'cultural hearth'* diffusion ..., whereby the innovation gains a foothold in both town and country in one particular region before diffusing to other parts of the country; and
- *'contra-hierarchical'* diffusion..., whereby innovations diffuse *against* the urban hierarchy, arising in rural areas and spreading to urban ones. (2009: 137–8, emphasis in original)

As we shall see, observed diffusion in England and the UK has tended to be of the first two types. In the following sections, I shall first review evidence for a number of consonantal variants which have been observed to be diffusing throughout most of Britain in the late twentieth and early twenty-first century. I shall then discuss the diffusion of morphosyntactic variants within England before considering the possibility of global diffusion.

5.3.2 The diffusion of consonantal variants

In recent years, there has been considerable interest, from both sociolinguists and the general public in Britain, in a number of consonantal variants associated with 'Estuary English' and assumed to be diffusing from London to the rest of the country (including, in some cases, parts of Wales and Scotland). These are: glottalisation, particularly of /t/; 'TH-fronting' (/f/ and /v/ for <th>in *think, brother* etc.); and labiodental /r/, often interpreted as a [w] by non-linguists. These features have been widely reported as spreading like wildfire amongst young people throughout Britain. As we saw in Chapter 1, the media are always quick to seize on any evidence that 'Estuary English' is swamping local accents in places distant from London, even when the evidence provided by sociolinguistic researchers tells a more complex story.

Trudgill describes the spread of glottalisation as 'one of the most dramatic, widespread and rapid changes to have occurred in British English in recent times' (1999b: 136). This has largely been represented as a result of diffusion from London and the South-East of England to urban areas further north and west in England, as well as some parts of Wales (Mees 1987). In fact, the spread of glottalisation seems to have involved a 'pincer movement', with evidence from the West of Scotland as early as 1860 (Andrésen 1968) and from London in the early twentieth century, so that glottalisation in Northern cities could well have arrived from further north rather than from London (see Beal 2007 for a historical account of this). Whilst acknowledging Andrésen's point about the early evidence from Scotland, Kerswill suggests that 'the feature seems to have diffused to urban centres outside the south-east within the last 30–40 years' (2003: 232). Whatever the precise origin or origins of glottalisation, there is overwhelming evidence for its diffusion in the late twentieth century. If we look at the chapters in Foulkes and Docherty (1999), we find the following accounts from a variety of locations:

- Sheffield: '[ʔ] is used for non-initial /t/ much more frequently by younger speakers' (Stoddart et al. 1999: 75)
- Derby: '[ʔ] is almost categorical for word-final /t/ before a consonant.

It is also the majority pronunciation where /t/ occurs pre-pausally, but significantly more so for young speakers ... The most marked sociolinguistic patterning occurs in pre-vocalic position ... where glottals occur only 9% of the time for older speakers, in contrast with 60% for younger speakers' (Docherty and Foulkes 1999: 50)

- Sandwell (West Midlands): 'The glottal stop is very frequent in teenage speech and also variably in young adult (30 yrs) speech ... but very infrequent in the speech of the elderly' (Mathisen 1999: 110)
- Hull: 'Older speakers in Hull use less glottal replacement of /t/ than younger people' (Williams and Kerswill 1999: 147)
- West Wirral: 'Pre-consonantal/final /t/ was often glottalised as it is increasingly in many areas' (Newbrook 1999: 97).

These accounts all point to an increase in the use of glottalised variants among younger people. Elsewhere, there is evidence that this diffusion is, or at least at some stage has been, of the 'urban hierarchical' type: in data collected in the 1970s, Petyt (1985) found evidence of glottalisation in the larger city of Bradford but not in smaller towns such as Huddersfield. However, a counter-example exists in the case of Liverpool. Although, as cited from Newbrook above, there is evidence of glottalisation in West Wirral, it is largely absent from Liverpool, which is the dominant city in this area. We will discuss this apparent anomaly further in Section 5.4.

TH-fronting, like glottalisation, has been widely observed in both popular and scholarly accounts of the speech of young people in England. The chapters in Foulkes and Docherty (1999) include the following comments:

- Newcastle: 'The labiodental forms [f, v] for /θ, ð/ can be found in younger, particularly WC [working-class] speech, but are still relatively scarce' (Watt and Milroy 1999: 30)
- Derby: 'The labiodental forms [f, v] for /θ, ð/ have made great inroads into younger WC [working-class] speech, such that all eight young WC speakers made at least one variable use of them, and three speakers even used labiodentals categorically in word-list readings' (Docherty and Foulkes 1999: 51)
- Sheffield: '[f, v] are possible realisations of the dental fricatives /θ, ð/ for younger speakers, particularly males, in medial and final positions' (Stoddart et al. 1999: 76)
- Sandwell (West Midlands): '[θ, ð] for adult speakers; [f, v] for an increasing number of teenagers and nearly categorical with boys' (Mathisen 1999: 111)
- Norwich: 'TH-fronting was completely absent from Norwich English

in 1968. By 1983, however, it had become very common indeed'
(Trudgill 1999b: 132)

- Milton Keynes, Reading and Hull: '/θ, ð / are realised as [θ, ð] by older
  speakers; [f, v] are increasingly used by younger speakers' (Williams
  and Kerswill 1999: 147)
- London: 'In the broader speech of both age groups, there is variable
  use of [f] and [v] for /θ/ and /ð/ ... There is ... no significant difference between the age groups with regard to these features, and it
  seems there has been no recent change' (Tollfree 1999: 172)

This evidence indicates that, whilst TH-fronting is an established
feature of London speech, it is a more recent innovation elsewhere, and
is only just beginning to be adopted in Newcastle. This points to a
pattern of wave or contagion diffusion whereby the feature is spreading
westwards and northwards from London. Kerswill (2003) confirms this
pattern by examining a wider range of historical and contemporary
evidence. The SED material has more instances of fronting of /θ/ to [f]
from the areas immediately surrounding London and Bristol than
anywhere else, and none north of the Wash, except for 'what must be a
lexically-determined use of [f] in the item *sheath*, which is found sporadi-
cally throughout the country'. Kerswill concludes from this that 'the
change had not reached northern England by the time of the SED' (2003:
234). Kerswill goes on to summarise evidence from a wide range of
studies conducted at various times, as well as 'personal approaches to
linguists familiar with local speech' (2003: 235), and concludes that
TH-fronting is adopted later the further north you go. Thus it is found in
Middlesbrough before Newcastle, in Derby before Middlesbrough, etc.
Kerswill also finds evidence for hierarchical diffusion: in the nineteenth
century the feature spread from London to another large port city,
Bristol, before it reached smaller towns in between, and more recently it
has been attested in the similarly sized cities of Derby and Norwich at
about the same time, but later in the smaller town of Wisbech. Finally,
Kerswill notes that, in more northerly locations, the innovation reaches
larger cities such as Newcastle and smaller ones such as Durham at the
same time and so cannot be described as diffusing from one to the other.
He suggests that in cases like this, where an innovation reaches a 'critical
mass ... it can spread by a process of both levelling and diffusion' (2003:
237–8).

The third consonantal feature which is often cited as a diffusing
innovation in British English and associated with 'Estuary English' is
labiodental /r/. Kerswill (2003: 231) mentions this alongside TH-fronting
and glottalisation as one of the 'torchbearers of geographical diffusion'.

However, the evidence from Foulkes and Docherty (1999) is more patchy in this case. Whilst both Watt and Milroy (1999: 30) and Docherty and Foulkes (1999: 51) describe this variant as increasingly used by young speakers in Newcastle and Derby, and Trudgill (1999: 133) reports it being used by 'one third of informants born between 1959 and 1973' in Norwich, Newbrook (1999: 98) and Mathison (1999b: 111) report few examples of this feature in West Wirral and Sandwell respectively. Foulkes and Docherty (2000) suggest that this variant could have been introduced into London English as a result of dialect contact with Yiddish-speaking immigrants in the nineteenth century, a scenario associated with levelling rather than diffusion. Labiodental /r/ is often perceived as a speech defect, and is common in the speech of young children, so it is possible that, despite its association with 'Estuary English', this feature is not diffusing from London, but is increasingly heard in the speech of young people throughout the country who are now less likely to be 'corrected' than their parents were. Britain comments on the fact that a number of the features reported to be diffusing widely are 'highly typologically unmarked forms ... and acquired early by most Anglophone children, unlike their standard counterparts' (2009: 139). He is referring here to TH-fronting and /l/-vocalisation, but the same could be said about labiodental /r/.

5.4 Resistance and divergence

5.4.1 Resistance and phonological structure

Although, as we have seen in Sections 5.2 and 5.3, there is a great deal of evidence for the processes of levelling and diffusion in England, there are also some notable examples of areas in which innovating features are not gaining ground, or even where regional varieties are diverging from those of surrounding areas. Britain makes the following observation about studies of diffusion and levelling:

> Much of the geolinguistic diffusion literature to date appears to suggest that the spreading innovation obliterates everything in its path, leaving a new dialectological landscape devoid of evidence of its past ... There has been an assumption that the process involves little more than 'a sequence of distributional changes' (Gregory 1985: 304) rather than a process which had locally specific outcomes, and which may be resisted both by local identity practices and local linguistic structural pressures. (2009: 139)

We will consider the effects of 'local identity practices' in the next chapter, but Britain's focus on 'local linguistic structural pressures' is pertinent to several apparent exceptions to the general trend for certain innovations to diffuse throughout the country. Johnson and Britain (2007) discuss the case of /l/-vocalisation, yet another feature of 'Estuary English' that has been observed to be spreading from its epi-centre in London. In Foulkes and Docherty (1999), /l/-vocalisation is noted as occurring in Derby (Docherty and Fouulkes 1999: 52), Sandwell (Mathisen 1999: 111), Reading and Milton Keynes (Williams and Kerswill 1999: 148) and, of course, London (Tollfree 1999: 174). In all these places, vocalisation is more frequent in the speech of young people, indicating a change in progress. However, there is no report of /l/-vocal-isation in Newcastle, Hull or Norwich, which contradicts the idea that this feature is diffusing geographically. As we saw in Section 2.2.7, one thing that the accents of Newcastle and Norwich have in common is the absence of clear/dark allophony in the /l/ phoneme: both have clear /l/ in all contexts. Johnson and Britain (2007) argue that vocalisation of /l/ is a natural development wherever there is clear/dark allophony, but that both these features are fairly recent innovations in British English:

> Vocalisation … will only take place, it seems, once the dialect in question has acquired a dark /l/ in (at least) syllable rhyme contexts. Dark /l/ in such contexts has only been widespread since the mid-19th century and so the vocalisation which, we claim, can naturally follow from it is, also, a relatively recent phenomenon of English dialects. (2007: 302)

Thus the diffusion of /l/-vocalisation is not, or at least not solely, due to factors such as prestige or the cultural prominence of London, but is a 'natural' sound change. Likewise, where the innovation has not spread, this is not due to the geographical isolation of Newcastle and East Anglia, but to the phonological structure of the accents of these places.

5.4.2 Divergence

We saw in Section 5.3.2 that Liverpool is one of the few urban areas in England where the spread of diffusing features, notably glottalisation and TH-fronting, has not been observed. Watson argues that 'certain aspects of Liverpool English (Scouse) pronunciation are resisting level-ling and that another is showing signs of moving, not *towards* a putative regional standard, but is in fact diverging from phonological norms' (2006: 55). In this paper, Watson uses the pronunciation of /t/ as a test case for whether the accent of Liverpool is moving in the same direction as other urban accents in England, resisting the innovation, or actually moving in a different direction. He notes that the earliest scholarly account of Liverpool English (Knowles 1973) mentions a phenomenon which Knowles refers to as 't elision'. Watson cites Knowles as stating that 'there is a small class of words including *get, got, bit, what, that, it, not* in which the final /t/ is sounded before another consonant but can be elided in final position' (Knowles 1973: 234, cited in Watson 2006: 56). Watson interprets this as referring not to glottalisation, since Knowles explicitly states that this is rare in Liverpool speech, but to what he calls 't > h', on the grounds that 'there is absence of both an oral gesture and a glottal closing gesture' and 'an audible release of breath' (2006: 86).

As we saw in Section 5.1, the process of levelling is defined as involving the reduction of marked variants. Since 't > h', at least within England, is uniquely found in the accent of Liverpool, it should be a prime candidate for levelling, especially, as Watson points out, since it is described by Knowles as occurring in exactly the position where glottalisation is used even by younger RP speakers. Watson compares the evidence presented in Knowles (1973) with that from a corpus of Liverpool speech collected from sixteen adolescents from the same area of Liverpool in which Knowles collected his data. The comparison of these two data sets would allow Watson to determine the direction of linguistic change with regard to this feature in the second half of the twentieth century. Watson finds that 'of all 945 tokens of pre-pausal /t/, there was not a single glottal stop' (2006: 59), thus confirming that this diffusing feature has made no inroads into the accent of Liverpool. So far, this could be seen as evidence of the kind of resistance noted by Britain (2009) and Johnson and Britain (2007) and discussed in Section 5.4.1 above. However, Watson finds that it is not just the case that the diffusing feature is resisted, but the 'marked' variant [h] is actually spreading to new contexts. Whilst Knowles had noted that what he called 't elision' was restricted to monosyllabic function words, Watson found that his adolescent subject also had [h] for pre-pausal /t/ in a number of polysyllabic words including *maggot, Robert, target, ticket* and *merit* and, indeed, that 't > h' occurred 100 per cent of the time in *biscuit, bucket* and *chocolate*. Watson concludes that 'Liverpool English is not, as the popular press would have us believe, losing its regionality, but instead is moving in the opposite direction and *diverging* from supra-local norms' (2006: 61).

Watson's results cry out for explanation: why are speakers in Liverpool behaving differently from those in the rest of England with regard to the pronunciation of /t/? The presence of 't > h' in this accent of English could be interpreted as evidence of Irish-English influence on the speech of the city, which, from the nineteenth century onwards, has had a larger number of Irish immigrants than any other in Britain

(Hickey 1999 notes 't > h' as a feature of Dublin English), but that still would not explain why such a marked feature is expanding rather than disappearing in the twenty-first century. The structural arguments put forward by Johnson and Britain (2007) and discussed in Section 5.4.1 with reference to resistance to /l/-vocalisation do not apply in this case. It would be tempting to argue that young Liverpudlians are behaving differently from their contemporaries in other towns and cities because they have such a strong sense of local identity, but the same could be observed of other cities where glottalisation is being adopted. A possible explanation is that the sociolinguistic meaning of glottalisation in other accents of English is already carried by 't > h' in Liverpool, so there is no incentive for young Liverpudlians to adopt glottalisation. In order to pursue such a line of thought, we need to consider the relationship between regional language variation and identity, which is the subject of the next chapter.

Exercises

Go to the British Library's sound archive http://sounds.bl.uk/ and choose 'Accents and Dialects'. This will give you access to recordings from the Survey of English Dialects, recorded in the 1960s, and from the Millennium Memory Bank, a set of oral history recordings made in 1999.

Using the 'Browse by County' facility, choose one recording either from the SED or from an older person recorded for the Millennium Memory bank, and one recording of a younger person from the Millennium Memory Bank. If possible, try to choose people of the same gender.

- Does the older speaker use a wider range of features specifically associated with the accent and dialect of the locality?
- Does the younger speaker use any of the features discussed in Chapter 5 that have been observed to be diffusing in England, e.g. TH-fronting, glottalisation, labiodental /r/?
- Try to find out something about the recent history of the place these speakers come from. What factors might have led to levelling and/or diffusion?

Further reading

The foundational study of dialect contact and levelling is Trudgill (1986), but the first major study of this phenomenon in England is reported in Kerswill and Williams (2000). Kerswill (2002, 2003) provide useful explanations of levelling and diffusion, while Britain (2002, 2009) provide accounts of diffusion with more input from human geography. Each of the papers in Foulkes and Docherty (1999) provides evidence of levelling in a different variety of British English.

6 Variation and identity

6.1 Introduction

In previous chapters I have, at various points, referred to studies which invoke the notion of identity in connection with specific features of accent or dialect. In Chapter 2, I cited Wells's statement that 'many educated northerners ... would feel it a denial of their identity as northerners to say BATH words with anything other than short [a]' (1982: 354). In Chapter 3, I referred to Moore's finding that the use of *were* with first and third person singular subjects, which might be considered a 'traditional' feature of Bolton dialect and therefore more likely to be used by older speakers, is used by adolescent girls as a marker of group identity. Finally, in Chapter 5, I reported Watt's suggestion that issues of identity may also play a part in the levelling of GOAT and FACE vowels in Tyneside English, where the shift towards the 'supra-local' monophthongs is most advanced amongst younger speakers who want to retain their local/regional identity but do not want to be associated with the old-fashioned 'cloth-cap-and-clogs' image of their parents (1998: 7).

All these examples imply that specific linguistic variants are associated in the minds of speakers and hearers with particular social characteristics. Where these involve regionality, they may correspond to the geographical distribution of the features concerned, but other factors such as modernness or group membership may be more relevant to the speakers concerned. Even where regional identity is specifically associated with a linguistic feature, as in the case of the 'Northern' short [a] mentioned by Wells, this association may not correspond precisely with the known geographical distribution of the feature. As we saw in Chapter 2, short [a] in BATH extends as far south as Birmingham, yet it is associated with Northern rather than Midlands identity in England. In this chapter, I will first review the ways in which sociolinguists have discussed and theorised identity and then go on to report on a number of recent studies of regional variation in England which have demonstrated how linguistic variants are used by speakers to signal identity.

6.2 Identity in early sociolinguistic studies

If we go back to the early days of sociolinguistics, we find that the prime motivation of scholars such as Labov was to find explanations for linguistic change. Whilst historical linguists had put forward structural explanations for certain changes, he pointed out that 'No change takes place in a social vacuum. Even the most systematic chain shift occurs with a specificity of time and place that demands an explanation' (Labov 1972: 2). In his early and much-quoted study of linguistic variation and change on the island of Martha's Vineyard, USA, Labov sought such an explanation for the distribution across the population of centralised variants of the diphthongs in words such as HOUSE (/aw/ in Labov's notation) and RIGHT (/ay/). Historically, these variants had been present in the variety of English brought over to the East Coast of the USA by seventeenth-century British settlers, and an earlier survey of the island for the *Linguistic Atlas of New England* (Kurath et al. 1939) showed that centralisation of /ay/ was very much in evidence, but that of /aw/ less so. Elsewhere in New England, the trend had been to move away from centralisation. When Labov correlated use of centralised diphthongs with the age of his participants, he found the seemingly counter-historical trend for every age-group except the youngest (14–30) to have more centralisation than the immediately older group, with the 31–45-year-olds demonstrating the highest level. This prompted Labov to ask the question 'Why should Martha's Vineyard turn its back on the history of the English Language?' (1972: 25).

Labov proceeded to correlate speakers' levels of centralisation systematically with social factors such as locality, occupation and ethnic group. This suggested that the speakers with the highest degree of centralisation were aged 31–45, residents of the 'Up-island' area and especially Chilmark, fishermen and of English ethnic origin, and Labov asked whether these social factors were 'truly independent from each other' or 'the result of some dependence on a larger factor which is logically prior to these' (1972: 26). In order to identify this 'larger factor', Labov provided a detailed picture of social and economic change on Martha's Vineyard.

This island is well known as a summer resort for the rich and famous, but at the time of Labov's survey it was in the late stages of a transition from an economy based on fishing to one based on tourism. As in many cases where wealthy incomers supplant the indigenous population and drive the price of housing beyond the means of the latter, this created resentment. Labov found that speakers with a high rate of centralisation tended to be those who expressed 'strong resistance to the incursions of summer people' (1972: 28). Since the traditional industry of the island was fishing, and Chilmark was the only place on the island where fishing was still economically important, the fishermen of Chilmark had become icons of 'traditional' island values, and this was reflected in their speech. Labov cites one such participant as saying:

> I think perhaps we use entirely different ... type of English language ... think differently here on the island ... it's almost a separate language within the English language. (1972: 29)

Labov suggested that the peak of centralisation in the 31–45 age group could be explained by the fact that this group of men were those under the greatest economic pressure: they were still breadwinners, but had joined the workforce at a time when the economy was in decline. These speakers would have had the greatest stake in identifying with 'traditional' island values: those of this age-group with less commitment to the island would have left for better prospects elsewhere and thus not be included in Labov's sample. When Labov correlated the degree of centralisation in the younger participants' speech with their stated intention of staying on the island or leaving, he found that the former showed high degrees of centralisation and the latter little or none. All this led Labov to conclude:

> the immediate meaning of this phonetic feature is 'Vineyarder'. When a man says [rɔɪt] or [həʊs], he is unconsciously establishing the fact that he belongs to the island: that he is one of the natives to whom the island really belongs. (1972: 36)

Here, Labov suggests that the association of centralisation with being a Vineyarder is unconscious, but he goes on to imply that there is a more conscious association:

> Centralized speech forms are then a part of the dramatized island character which the Chilmarker assumes, in which he imitates a similar but weaker tendency in the older generation. (1972: 37)

Furthermore, Labov goes on to explain that for the younger group, this image of the traditional Vineyarder 'will be ever present' and will form a reference point for those intending to stay on the island. He concludes that 'the meaning of centralization ... is positive orientation towards Martha's Vineyard' (1972: 38).

I have given a detailed account of this foundational study because it gives such a clear and persuasive example of the association of a linguistic feature with a very specific identity and set of values. We shall see how this kind of association is theorised and demonstrated in much more recent studies, but what has come to be known as Labovian sociolinguistics has tended to pay much less attention to identity as an explanatory factor in linguistic variation and change. Indeed, Labov himself appears to recant this emphasis on identity as an important factor in linguistic variation and change:

> The Martha's Vineyard study is frequently cited as a demonstration of the importance of the concept of local identity in the motivation of linguistic change. However, we do not often find correlations between degrees of local identification and the progress of sound change. (2001: 191)

The keyword here is *correlation*: the methodology developed by Labov in his study of English in New York City (1966) and applied and adapted to a British setting in Trudgill's study of Norwich (1974) involved the systematic comparison of social and linguistic variants with a view to establishing patterns linking the former with the latter. Typically, speakers from different social classes were found to behave according to a pattern whereby the higher the social class of the speaker, the more his or her speech would conform to the prestige norms of the speech community. Thus, in New York City, where, in line with General American speech it is more prestigious to pronounce /r/ in preconsonantal and word-final positions, the pattern was for speakers of higher social classes to have this rhotic pronunciation much more than those belonging to the lower social class groups. Likewise, Trudgill found that speakers in Norwich used the prestige (i.e. RP-like) pronunciation [ɪŋ] rather than [ɪn] for the -*ing* suffix in verbs such as *walking* according to their social class membership, as shown in Table 6.1. Each token of [ɪŋ] or [ɪn] was given a score of 1 for [ɪŋ] or 2 for [ɪn] and the average calculated, so that a high score indicates more use of [ɪn] and vice versa. The results show very clear stratification according to social class: the speakers in the highest social class group (middle middle class) use [ɪn] hardly at all and those in the lowest (lower working class) use it almost all the time.

Both Labov and Trudgill also found that speakers in the higher social class groups were more likely to 'shift' their speech patterns towards the prestige variants in more formal situations, such as reading out loud. Labov found that the one exception to this regular stratification of social classes and speech styles was the behaviour of the lower-middle-class speakers. They showed 'an extremely rapid increase, surpassing the upper-middle-class level in the two most formal styles' (1972: 115). Labov concluded that this 'crossover' pattern demonstrated the linguistic insecurity of the lower-middle-class speakers, and goes on to state:

Table 6.1 Social stratification of (ng) in Norwich (after Trudgill 1974: 92).

Social class	(ng) index score
Middle middle	3
Lower middle	15
Upper working	74
Middle working	88
Lower working	98

This linguistic insecurity is shown by the very wide range of stylistic variation used by lower-middle-class speakers; by their great fluctuation within a given stylistic context; by their conscious striving for correctness; and by their strongly negative attitudes towards their native speech pattern. (1972: 117)

Labov here is suggesting that the reason for the different speech patterns and styles used by speakers of different social classes can be explained by the notion of prestige: the lower-class speakers tend to conform to prestige norms less than their middle-class counterparts, but the lower-middle-class speakers 'outdo' their social superiors because they are 'insecure' about their position in society.

To explain why lower-class speakers persist in using forms which lack prestige in the speech community, Labov invoked the notion of 'an equal and opposing prestige for informal, working-class speech – a covert prestige enforcing this speech pattern' (1966: 108). He based this on the assumption that these speakers must want to speak the way they did, but he had no direct empirical evidence to support this. In his investigation of social variation in the speech of Norwich, Trudgill found such evidence. When asked what forms they used, working-class males tended to over-report their use of the non-prestigious variants. Trudgill attributed this to covert prestige and to the association of working-class values with the masculine traits of 'roughness and toughness' (1972: 183). He concluded:

Group-identification of a kind considered desirable by these speakers is signalled by the usage of the non-standard form, and this leads to its increase and exaggeration. Covert prestige, therefore, leads not only to the differentiation of the linguistic behaviour of the sexes, but also to the exaggeration of certain non-standard features, particularly by UWC [upper-working-class] and MWC [middle-working-class] men and by the young, which in turn leads to linguistic change. (1972: 192)

So here we see the notion of group identity invoked as an explanation for the linguistic behaviour of working-class males and the suggestion that linguistic variants are associated in their minds with blue-collar values. Lower-class speakers speak as they do not because their lack of exposure to educated norms has made them incapable of speaking any other way, but because their reference group – the set of speakers with which they identify and wish to be identified – is perceived as using the non-standard variants.

6.3 Theorising language and identity

6.3.1 The Labovian paradigm

As we have seen in the previous section, early sociolinguistic studies were concerned with finding explanations for linguistic change in the social stratification of linguistic variation. Labov went on to suggest that linguistic variables could be classified according to the ways in which they are evaluated by the speech community and the extent to which speakers are consciously aware of these evaluations. He postulated the following categories:

- *indicators*: these can be seen to vary according to some social characteristic, such as age, class etc., but are not subject to style-shifting and 'appear to have little evaluative force' (Labov 1972: 314);
- *markers*: these demonstrate both social and stylistic stratification. Speakers may not be consciously aware of these, but will respond to them systematically in subjective reaction tests, i.e. they will assume that speakers using the more prestigious variant are more educated, have better jobs, etc., and vice versa;
- *stereotypes*: these are forms which are prominently marked in the speech community and of which speakers are overtly aware. 'Stereotypes are referred to and talked about by the speech community; they may have a general label, and a characteristic phrase which serves equally well to identify them' (Labov 1972: 314).

The categories can be seen as representing different stages in linguistic change: an incoming form becomes an *indicator* when it has been adopted by all members of a subgroup; it becomes a *marker* when it has spread throughout the speech community and been assigned a common value by that community such that style-shifting will occur; finally, 'under extreme stigmatization, a form may become the overt object of social comment, and may eventually disappear. It is thus a *stereotype*, which may become increasingly divorced from the forms which are actually used in speech' (Labov 1972: 180). As an example of a stereotype which has disappeared from speech, Labov cites the inversion of /v/ and /w/ used by Dickens to characterise some of his Cockney characters. We know that this was a highly stigmatised feature of London English in the late eighteenth century because it is listed by the elocutionist John Walker as one of the 'peculiarities of … the Cockneys' (1791: xii), but Wyld (1936) claimed never to have heard it except as a joke. Today, it is not even recognised as a stereotypical feature of Cockney and is only known to readers of Dickens.

The problem with Labov's paradigm is that it assumes that stereotyping will be negative and that once speakers are overtly aware of a stereotyped variant they will avoid using it. However, what Labov termed 'covert prestige' can operate to preserve forms that are very overtly associated with social values. For example, the pronunciation [uː] for words which have [au] in RP (*house, now, town*, etc.) is recessive in Tyneside and 'confined almost exclusively to the speech of WC [working-class] males' (Watt and Milroy 1999: 29), but is more widely used in a few specific words, most notably *Toon*, meaning, not any old town, but Newcastle, or, increasingly, Newcastle United Football Club. The latter usage has been taken up by the national press, presumably for the sake of economy: a recent example is the headline 'Big decisions in a Toon, called malice' (*Guardian*, 15 August 2009, accessed 10 September 2009 at www.guardian.co.uk/sport/blog/2009/aug/10/newcastleunited-championship). It would be easy to dismiss this as just the kind of 'fossil' that Labov refers to as typical of the death-throes of a stereotyped variant, but in this case the fossilised usage is spreading rather than disappearing.

What is notable here is the association between a stereotyped variant and its usage in a word strongly associated with local identity. A similar phenomenon has been observed by Coupland in Cardiff, where the stigmatised 'Cardiff *a*' (/æː/) is found in all words in the phrase *Cardiff Arms Park* (formerly the Welsh national rugby stadium), and in the name of a local beer, *Brain's Dark*. In both the above cases the words which preserve stereotyped local pronunciations are those which refer to the cities themselves and to local icons. As Coupland puts it, 'regional pronunciation and local experience have a mutually encouraging, we might say symbiotic, relationship' (1988: 27). This would suggest that the relationship between linguistic variation and identity is more complex than Labov's prestige-based model suggests. Indeed, Labov has come to question the importance of prestige as a factor in linguistic change, stating that this is 'considerably weakened if the term "prestige" is allowed to apply to any property of a linguistic trait that would lead people to imitate it' (2001: 24). In the next section I shall put forward a language-ideology-based account of the relationship between linguistic variation and social values, which has been highly influential on recent studies of language and identity.

6.3.2 The language-ideological approach

The language-ideological approach was first introduced by Silverstein (1976) and developed by Agha (2003) and Lesley Milroy (2000, 2004). Silverstein posits three orders of indexicality whereby linguistic forms are associated with social categories:

- *first-order indexicality*: there is a correlation between a particular linguistic form and a social category, observable by an outsider such as a linguist;
- *second-order indexicality*: speakers come to rationalise and justify the link between the linguistic form and the social category. At this point their use of the feature becomes variable according to self-consciousness, identity, style, etc.;
- *third-order indexicality*: forms which have been linked with a certain social category become the subject of overt comment.

The orders relate to ascending levels of awareness within and beyond the speech community.

Whilst, as pointed out by Silverstein (2003) and Johnstone et al. (2006), the orders have some correspondence with Labov's indicators, markers and stereotypes, there is no implication that forms involved in third-order indexicality are liable to disappear as Labov predicted would happen to his 'stereotypes'. Indeed, third-order indexicality may lead to what Agha terms enregisterment, involving the identification of a set of linguistic norms as 'a linguistic repertoire differentiable within a language as a socially recognised register' which has come to index 'speaker status linked to a specific scheme of cultural values' (Agha 2003: 231). Due to a variety of discursive and metadiscursive activities, the latter involving what Johnstone et al. term 'talk about talk' (2006: 84), a particular set of features associated with an accent is 'enregistered' – represented collectively in the public imagination as a stable variety and maintained across time and region via practices that reiterate the value of the accent and its link to social status. Once it is fixed in place and time in this way, people can reflexively respond to a variety as a cultural value, and the repertoire of enregistered features can be used by speakers to express and/or perform identity. In this model, identity is viewed as a construct, and speakers/writers may take an active part in the process of enregisterment via such practices as dialect writing, the compilation of dialect dictionaries and, more recently, websites dealing with issues of dialect and local identity (see Beal 2009 for further discussion of this).

Since linguistic features have no inherent social meaning, individual features can be enregistered differently, i.e. represent different social values, for different groups of speakers. Thus in the history of English, alveolar [ɪn] for *-ing* has been associated with both upper-class (*huntin'*, *shootin'*, *fishin'*) and lower-class speech. In the UK, rhoticity is associated with the 'rustic' speech of the South-West, whereas in the USA it is prestigious. Even on a local level, a feature recognised by linguists as 'traditional' might index different values for different groups of speakers: to older speakers it might represent traditional or local values, but to adolescents it could index rebellion against institutional norms. For this reason, a number of sociolinguists have recently taken the view that identity should be directly investigated as part of the interview process, and have attempted to quantify identity data in order to produce correlations with linguistic variables. In the next section, I shall present a number of case studies which exemplify this approach.

6.4 Language and identity in England: case studies

6.4.1 Middlesbrough: a place with no identity?

Carmen Llamas's investigation of linguistic variation and change in the North-Eastern town of Middlesbrough provides a very clear example of a community in which 'local' identity has different meanings for different groups of speakers, who in turn express this identity via different linguistic variants. In order to investigate issues of identity in a systematic way, Llamas devised an identity questionnaire (IDQ), an extract from which appears in Figure 6.1.

Middlesbrough is a particularly interesting location for the study of language and local/regional identity because of its history, first as a nineteenth-century 'new town', and later as a place on the border of two major regions and with a complex recent history of reassignment to a succession of different local and regional authorities. Llamas cites a newspaper article in which Middlesbrough is described as 'pretty much a place between places ... a forgotten part of Britain with no identity' (*Sunday Times*, 5 March 2000, cited in Llamas 2007b: 580). As a new town of the industrial revolution, it is highly likely that Middlesbrough, or rather its inhabitants, would have had 'no identity' as a speech community. However, this was not quite what Trudgill (2004: 26) has termed a 'tabula rasa' situation because, even though Middlesbrough itself grew from almost nothing, there were English-speaking popula-

Your language

Q1 What accent would you say you had, and do you like it?

Q2 What would you think if your accent was referred to as 'Geordie' or 'Yorkshire'?

Q3 Can you recognise the accent of your home town (e.g. if heard on the radio or TV)? If so, how?

Your area

Q4 Can you remember when the county of Teesside was formed and Middlesbrough was no longer in Yorkshire? Do you think this made a difference.

Q5 Would you consider Teesside to be in a larger 'North-Eastern' part of the country or a larger 'Yorkshire' part of the country? Why?

Q6 If you were watching a regional news programme, what places would you expect to hear news from?

Q7 What do you consider the local football derby to be?

Figure 6.1 Extract from identity questionnaire (after Llamas 2007: 587).

tions in nearby towns and villages, so the variety of English that developed in Middlesbrough had characteristics in common with those of North Yorkshire, and indeed it was included in the county of Yorkshire until the local government reorganisation of 1968, alluded to in Q4 of Llamas's IDQ. Since then, the administrative boundaries affecting Middlesbrough have been redrawn a further three times. Whilst such reorganisations might seem purely bureaucratic exercises, Llamas found that the administrative shift out of Yorkshire was accompanied by a shift in cultural orientation away from Yorkshire and towards other North-Eastern cities such as Newcastle. Her investigation sought to establish whether this shift was accompanied by a reorientation of identity, and whether this in turn was signalled linguistically.

Answers to the IDQ did indeed point towards a shift in regional identity between the older generation, who had been born and raised when Middlesbrough was part of Yorkshire, and the youngest participants, who articulated a sense of Middlesbrough having an identity of its own, albeit within a broader 'North-East' region. Llamas found that older speakers most frequently gave the response 'Yorkshire' to Q1 ('What accent would you say you had?'), the middle-aged group tended to respond 'Teesside' and the young speakers most frequently responded with 'Middlesbrough'. In response to Q5, even older speakers who self-identified as 'Yorkshire' answered 'North-East', with one older speaker saying 'you're right at the top of Yorkshire, so to get it across you'd have to say North

East' (Llamas 2007b: 598). However, younger speakers' responses revealed what Llamas refers to as 'the irrelevance of Yorkshire to the speakers' sense of identity construction' (2007b: 598):

> It's weird even though you're the same distance, how much you don't class yourself with them [people from Yorkshire].

> It's weird when you only go two minutes down the road and you're in like North Yorkshire. No I don't consider it at all.

In response to Q2 ('What would you think if your accent was referred to as "Geordie" or "Yorkshire"?'), the oldest participants stated that they would be offended if misidentified as 'Geordie', but expressed surprise that this should happen. One participant responded 'I'm from Yorkshire not Geordieland – they might as well call you a Frenchman instead of an Englishman' (2007b: 598). The middle-aged group were more likely to prefer being misidentified as 'Geordie' rather than 'Yorkshire', but most of the young speakers claimed that they would be offended by being misidentified as a 'Geordie', and some expressed surprise that they might be misidentified as 'Yorkshire'. Thus the youngest speakers were identifying Newcastle and its inhabitants ('Geordies') as an out-group against which they defined their identity. This is further demonstrated by the responses to Q7 ('What do you consider the local football derby to be?'). The football derby, a match between teams from the same city or from neighbouring places, is one of the clearest manifestations of local identity and rivalry in Britain today. Llamas found that, whilst older participants saw Middlesbrough versus Leeds United as a local derby, the younger ones mentioned no teams from Yorkshire, but perceived matches against the North-Eastern teams Newcastle United and Sunderland as derbys.

In response to Q4 ('Can you remember when the county of Teesside was formed and Middlesbrough was no longer in Yorkshire? Do you think this made a difference?'), only the oldest participants expressed regret at leaving Yorkshire. The middle-aged tended to express uncertainty about their regional identity, with one stating 'we're not Geordie – we're not Yorkshire – we're nothing really' (Llamas 2007b: 600), but only one of the young participants expressed a desire to be part of Yorkshire, and some had no knowledge of any historical connection between Middlesbrough and Yorkshire.

Responses to Llamas's IDQ thus point very clearly to a shift in the orientation of local/regional identity between the three generations of her participants: the oldest affiliated themselves with Yorkshire, the middle-aged were uncertain about their identity but oriented more to the North-East region than to Yorkshire, and the youngest expressed a sense of a separate, Middlesbrough identity in opposition to that of Newcastle and perceived Yorkshire as having no relevance to their sense of identity. Llamas found that these shifts in local and regional orientation were reflected in linguistic variation and change between the generations. Her linguistic analysis concentrated on the plosives (p), (t) and (k), all known to be involved in variation and change elsewhere in the UK. A full glottal stop realisation of (t) is widespread throughout most of the UK, especially in younger speakers' usage, but 'glottal rein-forced variants' (Watt and Milroy 1999: 29-30) are characteristic of Tyneside speech. Neither the full glottal stop nor the glottal reinforced variants are traditionally found in the speech of Yorkshire (though the glottal variant of (t) is used by younger speakers here as elsewhere). We might expect, therefore, that orientation towards the North-East might be indexed by the use of glottal reinforced variants, whilst fully released stops might index a Yorkshire identity.

The results of Llamas's analysis bear this out to a certain extent: for (p) and (k), there was an overall increase in the use of glottalised variants by younger speakers, which, according to Llamas 'suggests a conver-gence of MbE [Middlesbrough English] with speech of farther north, where use of the glottalised forms was found to be higher' (2007b: 595). However, in the case of (t), the glottal rather than the glottalised variant had increased so as to be almost categorical for younger speakers of both genders. Since the glottal variant has been found to be less frequent in Tyneside English, this would appear to have the opposite motivation of diverging from the 'speech of farther north' and/or converging with the 'mainstream' UK vernacular.

After comparing the results of her linguistic analysis with the data from responses to the IDQ, Llamas interprets her findings as follows. The increase in the young speakers' use of glottalised variants of (p) could represent 'a convergent linguistic trend motivated by young speakers' positive identification with varieties of the North East', but the same speakers' responses to the IDQ indicate 'a shift not from Yorkshire to the North East but from Yorkshire to Middlesbrough' (2007b: 601). Since the glottalised variant of (p) was well established in Middles-brough, especially amongst male speakers, the shift towards this variant in young female speakers could be interpreted as indexing a 'Middles-brough' identity. Llamas concludes:

> We thus see a focusing of linguistic choices and convergence onto a Middlesbrough form, which coincides with the rise in profile of Middlesbrough as a place with its own identity in terms of local

administrative boundaries and in terms of perception of its prominence on a national scale. (2007b: 61)

Llamas goes on to interpret the increase in use of the glottal variant
of (t), in line with national trends and in contrast to Tyneside usage, as
consistent with the young participants' expressed desire to distinguish
themselves from 'Geordies'. Whilst older speakers still consider themselves as 'Yorkshire' and middle-aged ones are uncertain of their local
identity, younger speakers identify with Middlesbrough as a place and
index this identity in their use of linguistic variants of (p) and (t).

Llamas presents a very convincing case for treating identity as a
central concern in studies of linguistic variation and change. Without the
detailed qualitative data provided by responses to the IDQ, it would
have been easy to interpret the young Middlesbrough speakers' use of
glottal and glottalised variants as simply part of a wider regional or
national trend. In using the IDQ to 'deconstruct ... social identities',
Llamas demonstrates that the young speakers' linguistic behaviour
reflects the enregisterment of glottal reinforced (p) and glottal (t) as
'Middlesbrough' features indexing a specific local identity and 'used by
speakers to define and delimit a sense of self and to contrast themselves
with others in terms of the region in which they live' (2007b: 579).

6.4.2 Corby: a Scottish–English contact community

Dyer (2002) investigated the effects of dialect contact in the town of
Corby, Northamptonshire, where the construction of iron and steel
works in the 1930s led to large-scale immigration of workers from
Scotland, such that, by 1971, Scots accounted for a third of the town's
population. Although she did not construct an IDQ as such, Dyer
elicited comments about the town, its identity and its accent and used
these as qualitative data to explain the results of her linguistic analysis.
The expected outcome of the dialect contact is dialect levelling, but
Dyer found that this was not the case in Corby. She investigated two
vocalic variables with 'Scottish' and 'English' variants, THOUGHT and
GOAT. In the former, Scottish English has a merger with LOT, whereas
varieties of English spoken in areas surrounding Corby do not, and in the
case of GOAT, Scottish speakers have a monophthong in contrast with
various diphthongal variants found in the English Midlands, where
Corby is located. In the case of THOUGHT, Corby found a clear distinction between Scottish- and English-born speakers in the first (oldest) and
second generations of speakers, but the third generation, none of whom
had been born in Scotland, overwhelmingly used the English variants.

Dyer notes that 'these results suggest that the younger speakers are avoiding distinctly Scottish features in their speech and adopting established Anglo-English features' (2002: 106), an outcome that might be expected in a dialect contact situation. However, the results for GOAT pointed in a different direction: in the first generation, as might be expected, Scottish-born speakers used monophthongal variants of GOAT and English-born speakers produced diphthongs. However, some of the second-generation speakers of English ethnicity produced monophthongal realisations and, by the third generation, this trend had advanced such that nine out of eleven speakers produced monophthongs, with four of these using the monophthongal variant more that 50 per cent of the time. This trend towards using the 'Scottish' variant was strongest amongst young men: young women, in contrast both to their male counterparts and to older participants, were producing tokens of the variants [æʏ] and [æɪ], innovatory variants observed by Kerswill (1994) to be spreading in South-East England.

Dyer considers that 'the features of the new Corby dialect cannot be accounted for entirely within a dialect levelling framework' (2002: 109) because the pattern of variation observed for the GOAT variable demonstrates that, far from being 'levelled out', what was originally a minority and stigmatised variant is spreading. Rejecting the explanation that a 'traditional variationist account' would provide, i.e. that 'third generation men are indexing Scottishness in their use of historically Scottish variants' (2002: 109), Dyer turns to analysis of the participants' comments for a more locally nuanced solution. She points out that none of the third-generation men, even those producing the highest percentage of 'Scottish' realisations of GOAT, expressed any sense of having a Scottish identity. Although they were aware of the town's historic connection to Scotland and that many local families had Scottish roots, the younger men perceived no division between Scots and English in Corby. In response to the question 'At school are you conscious of who comes from a Scottish family and who doesn't?', one participant responded 'no not really we all speak the same around here' (2002: 111). The first-generation participants expressed an awareness of rivalry and division between Scots and English in Corby, but for the third generation the focus of rivalry and hostility was the nearby town of Kettering.

Dyer concludes that, whereas for first-generation speakers, monophthongal realisations of GOAT indexed Scottish ethnicity, for the third generation the same variant indexes a local, Corby identity in opposition to that of Kettering. The young women's adoption of innovatory, South-Eastern English variants, on the other hand, indexes a more outward-looking orientation. However, many young speakers in Corby use a combination of historically Scottish and English features, which Dyer interprets as showing that 'young Corby people possess the linguistic resources to project both more locally oriented and more outwardly oriented identities' (2002: 113). The employment of a language ideology model which takes account of participants' comments about language and identity has thus allowed Dyer to present a much more nuanced account of variation and change in Corby than would otherwise have been possible.

6.4.3 Sunderland: quantifying local identity

In her study of language and identity in the North-Eastern city of Sunderland, Burbano-Elizondo (2008) used an IDQ modelled on that employed by Llamas in order to obtain information about participants' sense of local identity. She went on to quantify the extent of participants' allegiance to Sunderland by means of an identification score index based on four factors: self-defining labels ('Mackem'[1]/'from Sunderland'/ other); attitude towards Sunderland (positive/neutral/negative); social activities (locally oriented/local and regional/outwardly oriented); and attitudes to local dialect (positive/negative). In each case, answers in the leftmost category ('Mackem', positive, locally oriented, positive) were assigned a score of 1, those in the middle category 0 and those in the rightmost category −1.

Burbano-Elizondo went on to correlate these identification scores with the participants' use of linguistic variants identified by the participants themselves and in popular publications as distinguishing the accent of Sunderland from that of Newcastle. One of these was 'H Dropping': whilst accounts of English accents traditionally locate the isogloss marking the northernmost limit of 'H Dropping' along the Tees, the perception within Tyne and Wear is that Mackems drop /h/ but Geordies do not. Burbano-Elizondo found that, whilst the extent of 'H Dropping' in the speech of her participants was minimal, it was still greater than that found in the speech of Tynesiders in the NECTE corpus. Furthermore, the extent of 'H Dropping' correlated with the Index of Sunderland Affiliation (ISA).

Table 6.2 shows the ISA scores for each of Burbano-Elizondo's participants. She points out the contrast between speakers on the extreme left and right sides of the table, where the ISA scores are lowest and highest respectively: on the left 'levels of usage of /h/-dropping are consistently low, ranging between 0% and 14.8%' whilst 'the speakers on the opposite end of the table, where the highest ISA scores are, display the highest frequencies of use of /h/-dropping within their speaker groups' (2008: 213). It would appear, then, that 'H Dropping' is used locally to index affiliation with Sunderland and opposition to Newcastle. Without recourse to the ISA as a means to quantify strength of local affiliation, all that a researcher would have noticed is that there is a slightly higher overall rate of 'H Dropping' in Sunderland than in Newcastle.

Table 6.2 Identification scores and percentage of 'H Dropping' (after Burbano-Elizondo 2008: 213).

| Index of Sunderland Affiliation (%) | | | | | | | | | | |
-4	-3	-2	-1	0	1	2	3	4	5	6
0			0	45			0			
			14.8							
	11.1				19.1		0			
					10	4.2				
0		0	0					0	22.2	
				19.2	3.3	4				20.8
										16.7
				0			0	0	40	
				17.9						
		0			17.4			13.04	55.2	
					15					

6.5 Conclusion

The three case studies discussed in Section 6.4 demonstrate the value of a language-ideological approach for studies of linguistic variation and change. In each case, linguistic variants are assigned local meanings and used to index identity in ways that can only be understood with reference to the participants' narratives of identity and opposition, whether these are obtained via a questionnaire or from more open-ended discourse. This ethnographic approach also has the advantage of allowing participants to speak for and identify themselves rather than be assigned to broad categories of social class, ethnicity, etc. Most of all, this approach views speakers as active agents in the creation and transmission of identity rather than passive victims of social forces. As Lesley Milroy states:

> An ideological analysis treats social categories as locally created by social actors and discoverable by analysis, rather than as a given. Consequently, an ideologically oriented account of language variation and change treats members of speech communities as agents

rather than as automatons caught up ineluctably in an abstract sociolinguistic system. (2004: 7)

It is worth noting that Labov's assertion cited above (p. 90), that 'we do not often find correlations between degrees of local identification and the progress of sound change' (2001: 191), predates the publication of the three studies outlined in Section 6.4. These and others taking a language-ideological approach demonstrate that 'degrees of local identification' do indeed correlate with linguistic variation and need to be taken seriously by sociolinguists.

Exercises

The identity questionnaire and identification score index below are adapted from Burbano-Elizondo's study of language and identity in Sunderland (2008: 61–3).

- Devise an identity questionnaire and identification score index relevant to your own location, using these as templates. For instance, if your location was between Manchester and Liverpool, question 1 on the identity questionnaire would be 'Do you consider yourself a Scouser, or a Manc, or neither?' If the location is not 'in between' places or has a less well-known identity label, you might ask: 'Is there a nickname for people from your town or city (such as Scouser for Liverpool or Geordie for Newcastle)? If so, would you use this word to describe yourself?'
- Answer the questions yourself, and try to get friends and family members to answer them (they will probably enjoy this).
- Use the identification score index to quantify the extent of their identification with their home town or city.
- Do these scores correlate with the extent to which they use features of local accent and/or dialect?

Identity Questionnaire

---

1 Do you consider yourself a Mackem, or a Geordie, or neither of them?

....

2 What accent do you think you have (e.g. Sunderland, Newcastle, Durham, etc.)?

....

3   Is your accent different from the accent of nearby cities such as Newcastle and Durham? Can you think of any specific ways in which it is different? For instance, are there any words which are pronounced differently?

....

....

4   Are you proud of your accent or would you rather not have any accent at all?

....

5   Would you prefer to have a different accent? If so, which one? Why?

....

6   Do you think it is good to have an accent? Why or why not?

....

7   Have you ever felt embarrassed about your accent? When? Why?

....

....

8   Are there different accents in the North-East? If there are, what are they? Do you like them? Can you tell them apart easily?

....

....

....

9   Where do you like going in your spare time within Tyne and Wear? What is your favourite shopping centre?

....

10 Which football team do you mainly support? Which team is its main rival?

....

....

11 What do you think of Sunderland as a city?

....

....

12 Do you think that Newcastle is generally more favoured than Sunderland, and because of that Newcastle tends to get the best facilities? Why or why not?

....

....

13 Who are generally more friendly, Newcastle people or Durham people? Why?

....

....

14 Is it necessary to speak with a Sunderland accent to be a Mackem?

....

15 What are the main reasons for the Geordie–Mackem rivalry?

....

....

16 Do you find it offensive to be called 'Mackem'? Why?

....

17 In the map of the North-East you have below, draw a line where you would place the boundary that separates the areas where Geordies and Mackems live.

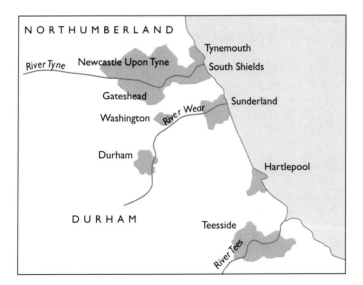

Identification Score Index

1 If you were on holiday and saw someone you had never seen before but who you thought came from Sunderland (e.g. you overheard their accent and recognised it, they were wearing the local football shirt), would you:
   (a) Feel compelled to go and ask where they were from and strike up a relationship?
   (b) Feel you had something in common but not do anything about it?
   (c) Not feel any differently from the way you would towards any other stranger?

2 Would you say you feel close to and you have something in common with people from Sunderland in general (that is, people you don't know personally), or would you say you don't feel any closer to them than to people from somewhere else?
   (a) Feel closer to people from Sunderland than to other people
   (b) Don't feel any closer to people from Sunderland than to other people
   (c) Don't know, can't say

3 Would you prefer your child's schoolteacher to have a local accent or not?
   (a) Prefer a person with a local accent
   (b) Prefer a person who spoke 'standard' English with a 'standard' accent
   (c) It wouldn't matter what accent they had

4 If you were voting in a local election, would the fact that a candidate was a local person persuade you to vote for them?
   (a) Yes, it would
   (b) No, it wouldn't
   (c) Don't know

5 If you wanted to leave something to a charitable organisation would you choose:
   (a) A local one
   (b) A national or international one
   (c) Don't know, depends on the cause

6 If there was a programme on TV about your home town which clashed with your favourite programme and you couldn't record either, would you:
   (a) Watch the programme about your home town and miss your favourite programme
   (b) Watch your favourite programme and miss the other (but wish you hadn't)
   (c) Watch your favourite programme and miss the other (but not mind)

Further reading

The place of identity in explaining language variation and change is a matter of contention amongst sociolinguists. For arguments against identity as a causative or explanatory factor see Trudgill (2004). Llamas and Watt (2010) is a collection of papers on various aspects of language and identity, several of which deal with British varieties and contexts.

Note

1. *Mackem* is a term for a citizen of Sunderland which was originally derogatory but has now been adopted by some of them. Its origin is unclear: local folklore associates it with the Wearside shipbuilding industry, but it also reflects the pronunciation of the word *make* south of the Wear. The first citation in the *OED* is from a Newcastle United fanzine from the 1980–1 football season, pointing to the origin of the term in local rivalry.

References

Agha, Asif (2003), 'The social life of cultural value', *Language and Communication*, 23: 231–73.

Aitchison, Jean (1997), *The Language Web: The Power and Problem of Words*, Cambridge: Cambridge University Press.

Anderwald, Liselotte (2002), *Negation in Non-Standard British English: Gaps, Regularizations and Assymetries*, London: Routledge.

Anderwald, Liselotte (2005), 'Negative concord in British English dialects', in Yoko Iyeiri (ed.), *Aspects of English Negation*, Amsterdam: John Benjamins, pp. 113–17.

Anderwald, Liselotte (2009), *The Morphology of English Dialects: Verb Formation in Non-Standard English*, Cambridge: Cambridge University Press.

Anderwald, Liselotte and Susanne Wagner (2007), 'FRED – The Freiburg English Dialect Corpus: applying corpus-linguistic research tools to the analysis of linguistic data', in Joan C. Beal, Karen P. Corrigan and Hermann L. Moisl (eds), *Creating and Digitizing Language Corpora. Volume 1: Synchronic Databases*, Basingstoke: Palgrave Macmillan, pp. 35–53.

Andrésen, Bjørn S. (1968), *Pre-glottalization in English Standard Pronunciation*, Oslo: Norwegian Universities Press.

Auer, Peter, Frans Hinskens and Paul Kerswill (eds) (2005), *Dialect Change: Convergence and Divergence in European Languages*, Cambridge: Cambridge University Press.

Batchelor, Thomas (1809), *An Orthoëpical Analysis of the English Language*, London: Didier and Tebbett.

Beal, Joan C. (1985),'Lengthening of *a* in Tyneside English', in Roger Eaton, Olga Fischer, Willem Koopman and Federike van der Leek (eds), *Papers from the Fourth International Conference on English Historical Linguistics*, Amsterdam and Philadelphia: John Benjamins, pp. 31–44.

Beal, Joan C. (1993), 'The grammar of Tyneside and Northumbrian English', in James and Lesley Milroy (eds), *Real English: The Grammar of English Dialects in the British Isles*, London: Longman, pp. 187–242.

Beal, Joan C. (1999), *English Pronunciation in the Eighteenth Century: Thomas Spence's 'Grand Repository of the English Language'*, Oxford: Clarendon Press.

Beal, Joan C. (2000), 'HappY-tensing: a recent innovation?', in Ricardo Bermudez-Ortero, David Denison, Richard M. Hogg and Christopher B.

McCully (eds), *Generative Theory and Corpus Studies*, Berlin: Mouton de Gruyter, pp. 483–97.

Beal, Joan C. (2004), *English in Modern Times 1700–1945*, London: Arnold.

Beal, Joan C. (2007), 'To explain the present: 18th- and 19th-century antecedents of 21st-century levelling and diffusion', in Jorge L. Bueno Alonso, Dolores González Álvarez, Javier Pérez-Guerra and Esperanza Rama Martínez (eds), *'Of Varying Language and Opposing Creed': New Insights into Late Modern English*, Bern: Peter Lang, pp. 25–46.

Beal, Joan C. (2008), 'English dialects in the North of England: morphology and syntax', in Bernd Kortmann and Clive Upton (eds), *Varieties of English 1: The British Isles*, Berlin: Mouton de Gruyter, pp. 373–403.

Beal, Joan C. (2009), 'Enregisterment, commodification, and historical context: "Geordie" vs. "Sheffieldish"', *American Speech*, 84(2): 138–56.

Beal, Joan C. and Karen P. Corrigan (2000), 'Comparing the present with the past to predict the future for Tyneside English', *Newcastle and Durham Working Papers in Linguistics*, 6: 13–30.

Beal, Joan C. and Karen P. Corrigan (2002), 'Relativisation in Tyneside and Northumbrian English', in Pat Poussa (ed.), *Relativisation on the North Sea Litoral* (LINCOM Studies in Language Typology, 7), Munich: Lincom Europa, pp. 125–34.

Beal, Joan C. and Karen P. Corrigan (2005a), 'A tale of two dialects: relativisation in Newcastle and Sheffield', in Markku Filppula, Juhanni Klemola, Marjatta Palander and Esi Penttilä. (eds), *Dialects across Borders*, Amsterdam: John Benjamins, pp. 211–29.

Beal, Joan C. and Karen P. Corrigan (2005b), '"No, nay, never": negation in Tyneside English', in Yoko Iyeiri (ed.), *Aspects of English Negation*, Amsterdam: John Benjamins, pp. 139–56.

Beal, Joan C. and Karen P. Corrigan (2007), 'Time and Tyne: a corpus-based study of variation and change in relativization strategies in Tyneside English', in Stefan Elspass, Nils Langer, Joachim Scharloth and Wim Vandenbussche (eds), *Germanic Language Histories from Below (1700–2000)*, Berlin: Mouton de Gruyter, pp. 99–114.

Britain, David (2001), 'Welcome to East Anglia! Two major dialect "boundaries" in the Fens', in Peter Trudgill and Jacek Fisiak (eds), *East Anglian English*, Woodbridge: Boydell and Brewer, pp. 217–42.

Britain, David (2002), 'Space and spatial diffusion', in Jack Chambers, Peter Trudgill and Natalie Schilling-Estes (eds), *The Handbook of Language Variation and Change*, Oxford: Blackwell, pp. 603–37.

Britain, David (2009), 'One foot in the grave? Dialect death, dialect contact and dialect birth in England', *International Journal of the Sociology of Language*, 196–7: 121–55.

Burbano-Elizondo, Lourdes (2008), 'Language variation and identity in Sunderland', PhD thesis, University of Sheffield.

Bybee, Joan L. and Carol L. Moder (1983), 'Morphological classes as natural categories', *Language*, 59: 251–70.

Cave, Andrew (2001), 'Language variety and communicative style as local and subcultural identity in a South Yorkshire coalmining community', PhD thesis, University of Sheffield.

Chambers, Jack and Peter Trudgill (1998), *Dialectology*, 2nd edn, Cambridge: Cambridge University Press.

Cheshire, Jenny (1982), *Variation in an English Dialect: A Sociolinguistic Study*, Cambridge: Cambridge University Press.

Cheshire, Jenny (2005), 'Syntactic variation and beyond: gender and social class variation in the use of discourse-new markers', *Journal of Sociolinguistics*, 9: 479–507.

Cheshire, Jenny and James Milroy (1993), 'Syntactic variation in non-standard dialects: background issues', in James Milroy and Lesley Milroy (eds), *Real English: The Grammar of English Dialects in the British Isles*, London: Longman, pp. 3–33.

Cheshire, Jenny, Viv Edwards and Pam Whittle (1993), 'Non-standard English and dialect levelling', in James Milroy and Lesley Milroy (eds), *Real English: The Grammar of English Dialects in the British Isles*, London: Longman, pp. 53–96.

Clifford, Sue and Angela King (2006), *England in Particular*, London: Hodder & Stoughton.

Coleman, Julie (2004), *A History of Cant and Slang Dictionaries: 1567–1784*, Oxford: Oxford University Press.

Cornips, Leonie E. A. and Karen P. Corrigan (2005), *Syntax and Variation: Reconciling the Biological and the Social*, Amsterdam: John Benjamins.

Coupland, Nikolas (1988), *Dialect in Use: Sociolinguistic Variation in Cardiff English*, Cardiff: University of Wales Press.

Dobson, Eric J. (1957), *English Pronunciation 1500–1700*, Oxford: Oxford University Press.

Docherty, Gerard and Paul Foulkes (1999), 'Newcastle upon Tyne and Derby: instrumental phonetics and variationist studies', in Paul Foulkes and Gerard J. Docherty (eds), *Urban Voices: Accent Studies in the British Isles*, London: Arnold, pp. 47–71.

Dolan, Terence P. (1998), *A Dictionary of Hiberno-English*, Dublin: Gill & Macmillan.

Dudman, Kate (2000), 'Loss of rhoticity and long mid monophthongisation in St. Ives, Cornwall', undergraduate dissertation, Essex University.

Dyer, Judy (2002), '"We all speak the same round here": dialect levelling in a Scottish–English community', *Journal of Sociolinguistics*, 6(1): 99–116.

Ellis, Alexander (1889), *On Early English Pronunciation, with Especial Reference to Shakespeare and Chaucer. Part 5: Existing Dialectal as Compared with West Saxon Pronunciation*, London: Trübner.

Ellis, Stanley (1953), 'Fieldwork for a dialect atlas of England', *Transactions of the Yorkshire Dialect Society*, 51(IX): 9–21.

Elphinston, James (1787), *Propriety Ascertained in her Picture. Volume II*, London: John Water.

Filppula, Markku, Juhani Klemola and Heli Pitkänen (eds) (2002), *The Celtic*

Roots of English, Joensuu: University of Joensuu.

Filppula, Markku, Juhanni Klemola and Heli Pitkänen (2008), *English and Celtic in Contact*, London: Routledge.

Finnegan, Ruth (1998), *Tales of the City: A Study of Narrative and Urban Life*, Cambridge: Cambridge University Press.

Fischer, Andreas (1976), *Dialects in the South-West of England: A Lexical Investigation* (Cooper Monographs, English Dialect Series 25), Bern: Francke.

Foulkes, Paul (2005), 'Sociophonetics', in Keith Brown (ed.), *Encyclopedia of Language and Linguistics* (2nd edn), Amsterdam: Elsevier, pp. 495–500.

Foulkes, Paul and Gerard J. Docherty (eds) (1999), *Urban Voices: Accent Studies in the British Isles*, London: Arnold.

Foulkes, Paul and Gerard J. Docherty (2000), 'Another chapter in the story of /r/: "labiodental" variants in British English', *Journal of Sociolinguistics*, 4(1): 30–59.

Giles, Howard and Peter Powesland (1975), *Speech Style and Social Evaluation*, London: Academic Press.

Glauser, Robert (1974), *The Scottish–English Linguistic Border: Lexical Aspects* (Cooper Monographs, English Dialect Series 20), Bern: Francke.

Glauser, Robert (1985), 'BOYS and GIRLS, SONS and DAUGHTERS: the evidence of the Survey of English Dialects', *English World-Wide*, 6(1): 37–58.

Görlach, Manfred (1999), *English in Nineteenth-Century England: An Introduction*, Cambridge: Cambridge University Press.

Gregory, Derek (1985), 'Suspended animation: the stasis of diffusion theory', in Derek Gregory and John Urry (eds), *Social Relations and Spatial Structure*, London: Macmillan, pp. 296–336.

Gresley, William S. (1883), *A Glossary of Terms Used in Coal Mining*, London: E. & F. N. Spon.

Harrison, Tony (1987), *Selected Poems*, 2nd edn, London: Penguin.

Hermann, Tanja, Lukas Pietsch and Susanne Wagner (2008), *A Comparative Grammar of British English Dialects*, Berlin: Mouton de Gruyter.

Heslop, Richard O. (1892), *Northumberland Words: A Glossary of Words Used in the County of Northumberland and on the Tyneside*, London: English Dialect Society.

Hickey, Ray (1999), 'Dublin English: current changes and their motivation', in Paul Foulkes and Gerard J. Docherty (eds), *Urban Voices: Accent Studies in the British Isles*, London: Arnold, pp. 265–81.

Honey, John (1988), '"Talking proper": schooling and the establishment of English "Received Pronunciation"', in Graham Nixon and John Honey (eds), *An Historic Tongue: Studies in English Linguistics in Memory of Barbara Strang*, London: Routledge, pp. 209–27.

Hughes, Arthur, Peter Trudgill and Dominic Watt (2005), *English Accents and Dialects*, 4th edn, London: Hodder Arnold.

Ihalainen, Ossi (1994), 'The dialects of England since 1776', in Robert Burchfield (ed.), *The Cambridge History of the English Language. Volume V*, Cambridge: Cambridge University Press, pp. 197–276.

Iyieri, Yoko (ed.) (2005), *Aspects of English Negation*, Amsterdam: John Benjamins.

Johnson, Wynn and David Britain (2007), 'L-vocalisation as a natural phenomenon: explorations in sociophonology', *Language Sciences*, 29: 294–315.

Johnstone, Barbara, Jennifer Andrus and Andrew E. Danielson (2006), 'Mobility, indexicality, and the enregisterment of "Pittsburghese"', *Journal of English Linguistics*, 34(2): 77–104.

Jones, Daniel (1909), *The Pronunciation of English*, Cambridge: Cambridge University Press.

Jones, Daniel (1917), *An English Pronouncing Dictionary, on Strictly Phonetic Principles*, London: Dent.

Jones, Jason (1998), 'Phonological and lexical change in the dialects of East Devon and West Somerset 1945–1995', PhD thesis, University of Wales Swansea.

Jones, Mark (2002), 'The origin of definite article reduction in northern English dialects', *English Language and Linguistics*, 6: 325–46.

Kerswill, Paul (1994), 'Babel in Buckinghamshire? Pre-school children acquiring accent features in the New Town of Milton Keynes', in G. Melchers and N.-L. Johannessen (eds), *Nonstandard Varieties of Language: Papers from the Stockholm Symposium*, Stockholm: Almqvist & Wiksell, pp. 64–84.

Kerswill, Paul (2002), 'Koinéization and accommodation', in Jack Chambers, Peter Trudgill and Natalie Schilling-Estes (eds), *The Handbook of Language Variation and Change*, Oxford: Blackwell, pp. 669–702.

Kerswill, Paul (2003), 'Dialect levelling and geographical diffusion in British English', in David Britain and Jenny Cheshire (eds), *Social Dialectology: In Honour of Peter Trudgill*, Amsterdam: John Benjamins, pp. 223–43.

Kerswill, Paul and Ann Williams (2000), 'Creating a new town koiné: children and language change in Milton Keynes', *Language in Society*, 29(1): 65–116.

Kerswill, Paul, Carmen Llamas and Clive S. Upton (1999), 'The first SuRE moves: early steps towards a large dialect project', in Katie Wales and Clive S. Upton (eds), *Leeds Studies in English*, Leeds: University of Leeds, pp. 257–69.

Kirkby, John (1746), *A New English Grammar, or Guide to the English Tongue*, London: R. Manby and H. S. Cox.

Knowles, Gerry (1973), 'Scouse: the urban dialect of Liverpool', PhD thesis, University of Leeds.

Kortmann, Bernd (2008), 'Synopsis: morphological and syntactic variation in the British Isles', in Bernd Kortmann and Clive Upton (eds), *Varieties of English 1: The British Isles*, Berlin: Mouton de Gruyter, pp. 478–95.

Kortmann, Bernd and Clive Upton (eds) (2008), *Varieties of English 1: The British Isles*, Berlin: Mouton de Gruyter.

Kortmann, Bernd, Tanja Hermann, Lukas Pietsch and Susanne Wagner (2005), *A Comparative Grammar of British English Dialects: Agreement, Gender, Relative Clauses*, Berlin: Mouton de Gruyter.

Kurath, Hans, Miles L. Hanley, Bernard Bloch, Guy S. Lowman Jnr and Marcus L. Hansen (eds) (1939), *Linguistic Atlas of New England*, Providence, RI: Brown University.

Labov, William (1966), *The Social Stratification of English in New York City*, Washington, DC: Center for Applied Linguistics.

Labov, William (1972), *Sociolinguistic Pattern*, Oxford: Blackwell.

Labov, William (2001), *Principles of Linguistic Change. Volume 2: Social Factors*, Oxford: Blackwell.

Llamas, Carmen (1999), 'A new methodology: data elicitation for social and regional language variation studies', *Leeds Working Papers in Phonetics and Linguistics*, 7: 95–118.

Llamas, Carmen (2007), 'A place between places: language and identities in a border town', *Language in Society*, 36(4): 579–604.

Llamas, Carmen and Dominic Watt (eds) (2010), *Language and Identities*, Edinburgh: Edinburgh University Press.

McDonald, Christine (1981), 'Variation in the Use of Modal Verbs with Special Reference to Tyneside English', PhD thesis, Newcastle University.

McDonald, Christine and Joan C. Beal (1987), 'Modal verbs in Tyneside English', *Journal of the Atlantic Provinces Linguistic Association*, 9: 42–55.

Mathisen, A. G. (1999), 'Sandwell, West Midlands: ambiguous perspectives on gender patterns and models of change', in Paul Foulkes and Gerard J. Docherty (eds), *Urban Voices: Accent Studies in the British Isles*, London: Arnold, pp. 107–23.

Mees, Inger (1987), 'Glottal stop as a prestigious feature in Cardiff English', *English World-Wide*, 8(1): 25–39.

Milroy, James and Lesley Milroy (1982), *Sociolinguistic Variation and Linguistic Change in Belfast*, London: Social Science Research Council.

Milroy, James and Lesley Milroy (eds) (1993), *Real English: The Grammar of English Dialects in the British Isles*, London: Longman.

Milroy, Lesley (2000), 'Two nations divided by the same language (and different language ideologies)', *Journal of Linguistic Anthropology*, 9(1): 1–34.

Milroy, Lesley (2004), 'Language ideologies and linguistic change', in Carmen Fought (ed.), *Sociolinguistic Variation: Critical Reflections*, Oxford: Oxford University Press, pp. 161–77.

Montgomery, Chris (2006), 'Northern English dialects: a perceptual approach', PhD thesis, University of Sheffield.

Moore, Emma (2003), 'Learning style and identity: a sociolinguistic analysis of a Bolton high school', PhD thesis, University of Manchester.

Morris, Marmeduke C. F. (1892), *Yorkshire Folk-Talk: With Characteristics of Those Who Speak it in the North and East Ridings*, London: Henry Frowde.

Mugglestone, Lynda (1995), *'Talking Proper': The Rise of Accent as a Social Symbol*, Oxford: Clarendon Press.

Nevalainen, Terttu (2006), *An Introduction to Early Modern English*, Edinburgh: Edinburgh University Press.

Nevalainen, Terttu and Helena Raumolin-Brunberg (2003), *Historical Sociolinguistics: Language Change in Tudor and Stuart England*, London: Longman.

Newbrook, Mark (1999), 'West Wirral: norms, self-reports and usage', in Paul Foulkes and Gerard J. Docherty (eds), *Urban Voices: Accent Studies in the British Isles*, London: Arnold, pp. 90–123.

Newbolt, Henry (1921), *The Teaching of English in England*, London: HMSO.

Orton, Harold (1930), 'The dialects of Northumberland', *Transactions of the Yorkshire Dialect Society*, 5: 14–25.

Orton, Harold (1933), *The Phonology of a South Durham Dialect: Descriptive, Historical and Comparative*, London: Kegan Paul.

Orton, Harold (1960), 'An English dialect survey: Linguistic Atlas of England', *Orbis: Bulletin International de Documentation Linguistique*, IX(2): 331–48.

Orton, Harold and Natalia Wright (1974), *A Word Geography of England*, London and New York, San Francisco: Seminar Press.

Orton, Harold, Stewart Sanderson and John Widdowson (eds) (1978), *The Linguistic Atlas of England*, London: Croom Helm.

Parish, William D. (1875), *A Dictionary of the Sussex Dialect and Collection of Provincialisms in Use in the County of Sussex*, Lewes: Farncombe.

Petyt, K. Malcolm (1985), *Accent and Dialect in Industrial West Yorkshire*, Amsterdam and Philadelphia: John Benjamins.

Quirk, Randolph, Sidney Greenbaum, Geoffrey Leech and Jan Svartvik (1985), *A Comprehensive Grammar of the English Language*, London: Longman.

Richards, Hazel (2008), 'Mechanisms, motivations and outcomes of change in Morley (Leeds) English', PhD thesis, University of York.

Romaine, Suzanne (1982), *Socio-Historical Linguistics: Its Status and Methodology*, Cambridge: Cambridge University Press.

Roper, Jonathan (2004), 'The etymology of *Gob, Gab* "mouth"', *Lore and Language*, 17: 65–6.

Samuels, Michael (1985), 'The Great Scandinavian Belt', in Roger Eaton, Olga Fischer, Willem Koopman and Federike van der Leek (eds), *Papers from the Fourth International Conference on English Historical Linguistics*, Amsterdam and Philadelphia: John Benjamins, pp. 269–81.

Sebba, Mark (2008), 'British Creole: morphology and syntax', in Bernd Kortmann and Clive Upton (eds), *Varieties of English 1: The British Isles*, Berlin: Mouton de Gruyter, pp. 463–77.

Shorrocks, Graham (1999), *A Grammar of the Dialect of the Bolton Area. Part II: Morphology and Syntax*, Frankfurt: Peter Lang.

Silverstein, Michael (1976), 'Shifters, linguistic categories and cultural description', in Keith H. Basso and Henry A. Selby (eds), *Meaning in Anthropology*, Albuquerque: University of New Mexico Press, pp. 11–55.

Silverstein, Michael (2003), 'Indexical order and the dialectics of sociolinguistic life', *Language and Communication*, 23: 193–229.

Simmelbauer, Andrea (2000), *The Dialect of Northumberland: A Lexical Investigation*, Heidelberg: Winter.

Stoddart, Jana, Clive Upton and John D. A. Widdowson (1999), 'Sheffield dialect in the 1990s: Revisiting the concept of NORMS', in Paul Foulkes and Gerard J. Docherty (eds), *Urban Voices: Accent Studies in the British Isles*, London: Arnold, pp. 72–89.

Stuart-Smith, Jane, Claire Timmins and Fiona Tweedie (2007), 'Talkin' Jockney: accent change in Glaswegian', *Journal of Sociolinguistics*, 11: 221–61.

Tagliamonte, Sali A. (1998), '"Was/were" variation across the generations: view from the city of York', *Language Variation and Change*, 10(2): 153–92.

Tagliamonte, Sali A. and Rika Ito (2002), 'Think really different: continuity and specialization in the English adverbs', *Journal of Sociolinguistics*, 6(2): 236–66.

Tagliamonte, Sali A. and Helen Lawrence (2000), 'I used to dance, but I don't dance now: the habitual past in English', *Journal of English Linguistics*, 28(4): 324–53.

Tagliamonte, Sali A. and Jennifer Smith (2002), 'Either it isn't or it's not: NEG/AUX contraction in British dialects', *English World-Wide*, 23(2): 251–81.

Tagliamonte, Sali A. and Jennifer Smith (2005), 'No momentary fancy! The zero complementizer in English dialects', *English Language and Linguistics*, 9(2): 1–12.

Tagliamonte, Sali A. and Jennifer Smith (2006), 'Layering, competition and a twist of fate: deontic modality in dialects of English', *Diachronica*, 23: 341–80.

Tagliamonte, Sali A., Jennifer Smith and Helen Lawrence (2005), 'No taming the vernacular! Insights from the relatives in northern Britain', *Language Variation and Change*, 17(1): 75–112.

Taylor, Francis E. (1901), *The Folk-Speech of Lancashire*, Manchester: John Heywood.

Tollfree, Laura (1999), 'South East London English: discrete *versus* continuous modelling of consonantal reduction' in change', in Paul Foulkes and Gerard J. Docherty (eds), *Urban Voices: Accent Studies in the British Isles*, London: Arnold, pp. 163–84.

Trudgill, Peter (1974), *The Social Differentiation of English in Norwich*, London: Cambridge University Press.

Trudgill, Peter (1986), *Dialects in Contact*, Oxford: Blackwell.

Trudgill, Peter (1990), *The Dialects of England*, 1st edn, Oxford: Blackwell.

Trudgill, Peter (1994), *Dialects*, London: Routledge.

Trudgill, Peter (1999a), *The Dialects of England*, 2nd edn, Oxford: Blackwell.

Trudgill, Peter (1999b), 'Norwich: endogenous and exogenous change', in Paul Foulkes and Gerard J. Docherty (eds), *Urban Voices: Accent Studies in the British Isles*, London: Arnold, pp. 124–40.

Trudgill, Peter (2003), *The Norfolk Dialect*, Cromer: Poppyland.

Trudgill, Peter (2004), *New-Dialect Formation: The Inevitability of Colonial Englishes*, Edinburgh: Edinburgh University Press.

Trudgill, Peter (2008), 'The dialect of East Anglia: morphology and syntax', in Bernd Kortmann and Clive Upton (eds), *Varieties of English 1: The British Isles*, Berlin: Mouton de Gruyter, pp. 404–16.

Trudgill, Peter and Jack Chambers (eds) (1991), *Dialects of English: Studies in Grammatical Variation*, London: Longman.

Upton, Clive S. and John D. A. Widdowson (1996), *An Atlas of English Dialects*, Oxford: Oxford University Press.

Upton, Clive S. and John D. A. Widdowson (1999), *Lexical Erosion in English Dialects*, Sheffield: National Centre for English Cultural Tradition.

Upton, Clive S., David Parry and John D. A. Widdowson (1994), *Survey of English*

Dialects: The Dictionary and Grammar, London: Routledge.

Upton, Clive S., Stewart Sanderson and John D. A. Widdowson (1987), *Word Maps: A Dialect Atlas of England*, London: Croom Helm.

Viereck, Wolfgang (1986), 'Dialectal speech areas in England: Orton's lexical evidence', in Dieter Kastovsky and A. Szwedek (eds), *Linguistics across Historical and Geographical Boundaries: In Honour of Jacek Fisiak on his Fiftieth Birthday. Volume I: Linguistic Theory and Historical Linguistics* (Trends in Linguistics, Studies and Monographs 32), Berlin: Mouton de Gruyter, pp. 725–40.

Vivian, Louisa (2000), '(r) in Accrington', undergraduate dissertation, Essex University.

Wagner, Susanne (2008), 'English dialects in the South-West: morphology and syntax', in Bernd Kortmann and Clive Upton (eds), *Varieties of English 1: The British Isles*, Berlin: Mouton de Gruyter, pp. 417–39.

Wakelin, Martyn F. (1977), *English Dialects: An Introduction*, London: Athlone.

Wakelin, Martyn F. (1983), 'The stability of English dialect boundaries', *English World-Wide*, 4(1): 1–15.

Wales, Katie (2003–4), 'Second person pronouns in contemporary English: the end of a story or just the beginning?', *Franco-British Studies*, 33–4: 172–85.

Wales, Katie (2006), *Northern English: A Social and Cultural History*, Cambridge: Cambridge University Press.

Walker, John (1791), *A Critical Pronouncing Dictionary*, London: G. G. J. and G. Robinson and T. Cadell.

Watson, Kevin (2006), 'Phonological resistance and innovation in the North-West of England', *English Today*, 86(22/2): 55–61.

Watt, Dominic (1998), 'Variation and change in the vowel system of Tyneside English', PhD thesis, Newcastle University.

Watt, Dominic (2002), '"I don't speak with a Geordie accent, I speak, like, the Northern accent": contact-induced levelling in the Tyneside vowel system', *Journal of Sociolinguistics*, 6(1): 44–63.

Watt, Dominic and Lesley Milroy (1999), 'Variation in three Tyneside vowels: is this dialect levelling?', in Paul Foulkes and Gerard J. Docherty (eds), *Urban Voices: Accent Studies in the British Isles*, London: Arnold, pp. 25–46.

Wells, John C. (1982), *Accents of English*, Cambridge: Cambridge University Press.

Williams, Ann and Paul Kerswill (1999), 'Dialect levelling: change and continuity in Milton Keynes, Reading and Hull', in Paul Foulkes and Gerard J. Docherty (eds), *Urban Voices: Accent Studies in the British Isles*, London: Arnold, pp. 141–62.

Williams, Michael (1991), 'Post-vocalic (r) in the urban speech of the Isle of Wight', *Wellington Working Papers in Linguistics*, 3: 56–66.

Wright, Joseph (1898–1905), *The English Dialect Dictionary*, London: Frowde.

Wright, Joseph (1905), *The English Dialect Grammar*, Oxford: Frowde.

Wright, Peter (1972), 'Coal-mining language: a recent investigation', in Martyn F. Wakelin (ed.), *Patterns in the Folk Speech of the British Isles*, London: Athlone, pp. 32–49.

Wyld, Henry C. (1936), *A History of Modern Colloquial English*, 3rd edn, Oxford: Blackwell.

Websites

BBC Voices, www.bbc.co.uk/voices

British Library sound archive, http://sounds.bl.uk

Common Ground, www.commonground.org.uk/distinctiveness/d-index.html

Estuary English (John Wells), www.phon.ucl.ac.uk/home/estuary

Newcastle Electronic Corpus of Tyneside English (NECTE), www.ncl.ac.uk/necte

Northumbrian Language Society, www.northumbriana.org.uk/langsoc

Oxford English Dictionary, www.oed.com

Sounds Familiar (British Library), www.bl.uk/learning/langlit/sounds

The Guardian, www.guardian.co.uk

This is Derbyshire, www.thisisderbyshire.co.uk/dialect

UNESCO Convention for the Safeguarding of Intangible Cultural Heritage, www.unesco.org/culture/ich_convention/index.php?pg=00003

Index